Remarks Upon North Wales
by William Hutton

Copyright © 2019 by HardPress

Address:
HardPress
8345 NW 66TH ST #2561
MIAMI FL 33166-2626
USA
Email: info@hardpress.net

CVB
Hotton

CLUB

THE NEW YORK
PUBLIC LIBRARY

ASTOR, LENOX AND
TILDEN FOUNDATIONS
R   L

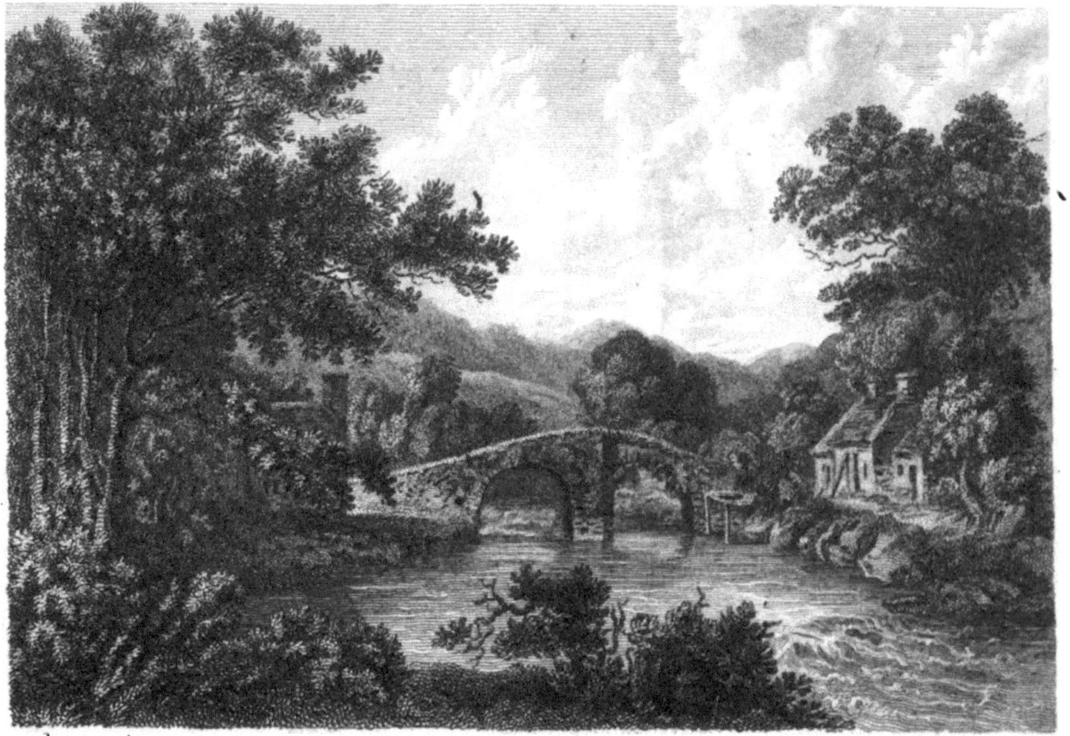

Barber del.

J. Landseer direx.

Beddkelert.

REMARKS UPON

NORTH WALES,

BEING THE RESULT OF

SIXTEEN TOURS

THROUGH THAT PART OF THE

PRINCIPALITY.

By W. HUTTON, F. A. S. S. Birmingham.

EMBELLISHED WITH

Frontispiece View of Beddkelart, and three Etchings of some of the principal mountainous Views.

BIRMINGHAM,
PRINTED FOR, AND SOLD BY KNOTT & LLOYD,
AND ALSO SOLD BY L. B. SEELEY, and VERNOR & HOOD, LONDON,
And by every other Bookseller in the United Kingdom.

Printed at the Office of the Executors of T. A. Pearson.

1803.

TO THE RIGHT HONORABLE
LORD PENRHYN.

MY LORD,

IT is not from pecuniary views that *I* address you, for *I* am, and probably shall continue, a stranger. Interest can have no weight with him who has enough; for we do not estimate a man's finances by what he has, but by what he wants.—*I only solicit what I believe you will grant, a pardon for the liberty I have now taken.*

My sole motive is, to ingraft praise upon merit. When I see a man furnishing the world with real riches, I cannot view his proceedings with an indifferent eye. I feel sentiments of beneficence. It may be asked, What are real riches? The answer is easy: It is not gold

gold or silver (he can eat neither) but that which is the support of man, the produce of the earth. *He can dine upon a* loaf, *and a* steak; *the issues of cultivated land; but he cannot dine upon a* guinea, *or, its false substitute,* a bank note. *These are of little value in themselves, although, by general consent, they are become the medium to ascertain the value of others.*

It is for you, my Lord, to cause riches of the most valuable kind to rise from the earth, to call dead land into life, to rescue the meadow from drowning, teach growth to the steril field, reduce the rocks, and fertilize the hills. Thus, by your aid, man is supported; and by your example, which is the greatest of all charity, he is taught to support himself.

I am, My Lord,
    Your obedient Servant,
        W. HUTTON.

PREFACE.

IN former ages, the English rarely entered Wales but to destroy it. Her sovereign mountains, beautiful vallies, and surprising cascades, instead of being admired, were tinged with blood. Nor was the eye of the curious fascinated with her wonders till within the last fifty years. The improvement of her roads, and particularly the daily communications between England and Ireland, brought her into notice.

The English traveller, at length, ventured to climb her precipices, descend

descend her glens, and admire her curiosities, and now the vast influx of annual visitants enrich her with their wealth. If the fathers oppressed her, their children support her.

Though the world is frequently favoured with WELCH TOURS; yet the historical knowledge is but in its infancy.----If much *is* said, much remains.

I follow the footsteps of no author, but make those remarks only which fell under my own eye, in travelling sixteen times, in various directions, through that principality.

CONTENTS.

CONTENTS.

CHAP. I.

Ludlow—Bishop's Castle—Offa's Dyke—Montgomery—New Town—Llanidloes—Sputty—Devil's Bridge—Aberistwith—Malwyd—Canoffice—Llanvair—Welch Pool.

CHAP. II.

Malwyd—Dinas Mouddy—The Yew—The Cottage—Head of two Rivers—Cader Idris—Dolgelly—Barmouth—The Welch Language—Eglwys Wrw—Bala—Pont y Glyn.

CHAP. III.

REMARKS IN
A TOUR THROUGH WALES,
In August, September, and October, 1797.

The Wrekin—Oswestry and Oswald—Llangollen—Owen Glendwr—Caractacus—Keniogie—Llanrwst—Conway—Aber—Rhiaidr Mowr—Way to find Sunday—Bangor—Virtues of Plum Pudding—Caernarvon—Welch Wedding—The Jumpers—Journey from Birmingham.

CHAP. IV.
DINAS DINLLE.

CHAP. V.
CLYNOG.

CHAP.

CHAP. VI.

LLYNIEU NANDLE
AND
DRWS Y COED.

CHAP. VII.

Capel Cerig—Glyn Llugwy—Rhaiadr y Wenol—Bettws y Coed—The Conway—Festiniog—Cross Hour—Beddkelart—The Land-Water—The Goat—Old Caernarvon.

CHAP. VIII.

SNOWDON.

CHAP. IX.

Dol Badern Castle—Llanberris—Bwlch y Gwyddil—Bwlch yr Eisteddfa—Roads—Nant Gwynan—Nant Frankon.

CHAP. X.

The Ferries—Druidical Remains—Bryn Gwyn—Astronomer's Stone—Tre'r Drwr Bach—Tre'r Dryw—Tan Ben y Cefn—Llanidan—The Carnedd—The Cromlech—Owen Tudor—Beaumaris.

CHAP. XI.

St. Asaph—Denbigh—Ruthin—Mold—Offa's Dyke.

REMARKS UPON WALES, &c.

CHAP. I.

Ludlow—Bishop's Castle—Offa's Dyke—Montgomery—New Town—Llanidloes—Sputty—Devil's Bridge—Aberistwith—Mallwyd—Canoffice—Llanvair—Welch Pool.

THE recovery of the health of her I loved, was the cause of my first visiting Wales. I hoped benefit would arise from exercise of some length, amusement, and sea air. We therefore, with my daughter, fixed upon Aberistwith, and set out in a rainy season, about the 25th of July, 1787.

B LUDLOW.

LUDLOW.

Passing through Ludlow, I thought it abounded with female beauty; but every place exhibits handsome women when dressed for church on Sunday.

BISHOP's CASTLE.

We slept at Bishop's Castle, so called from a castle upon an elevated spot, now a bowling-green, where the bishops of Hereford resided. It is a manor, and a borough, chiefly consisting of one street, cost Lord Clive 35,000l. and brings into the pocket about 2000l. a year, and two members into the House of Commons.

OFFA's DYKE.

Four miles beyond we crossed Offa's Dyke, the famous division between England and Wales. I quitted the chaise to examine it. There seems to be about twenty yards space

between

between the summit of each bank, and I suppose it has been about six deep, now half as much. This view has ever since excited a wish, which will never be gratified, to travel from one end to the other, about a hundred and thirty miles.

MONTGOMERY.

Upon an eminence we had a view of the beautiful vale of Montgomery, ten miles over, terminated with Powis Castle. The town of Montgomery is small, compact, and lies under a hill, which, when we mounted, we almost seemed to climb over the houses.

NEW TOWN

Had but one inn, and one chaise, nor was there another between that and Aberistwith, forty-four miles. The landlord insisted upon his own price, on running four horses, and two postillions, and as we could go to no other market, we were obliged to comply. We gave him

him a promise to visit him no more, nor have we broken that promise.

LLANIDLOES.

We reposed that night at Llanidloes, a smart town of about two hundred houses. Here I first heard the Welch tongue, and here we had a rainy evening, but the last rain till my return home.

Aberistwith was now distant thirty miles, many of which were over sheep walks, nearly without sheep or inhabitants; for not a dwelling appeared, except a distant cottage or two, without light, and without land, inhabited by shepherds.

SPUTTY.

There was only one inn upon the road, Sputty, and that produced neither entertainment for man or horse, except a chair for the one, and a stable for the other. There are now both. Here we stopped two hours to rest;

rest; our entertainment was a quarrel between our host and hostess, who had, in advanced life, married a second time, when the powers of affection were gone, and, instead of one spark of love warming the breast of either, the flames of hatred were ready to consume both. The only pleasure found in matrimony was, in each blazoning the errors of the other to all comers. Death is sometimes wished for by *one*, but here by *two*.

DEVIL's BRIDGE.

Proceeding a mile further, we came to one of the wonders of Wales, the Devil's Bridge (Pont Mynach) much resembling Pont y Glyn, in the road between Corwen and Cernioge, but upon a larger scale. I had the pleasure of seeing it in great perfection, being immediately after heavy rains.

The reader, who has not travelled over it, may figure to his idea, a rock nearly even with the turnpike road, cleft transverse to the depth of ninety-nine feet close to the bridge on one side, and one hundred and fourteen on the other, consequently the water falls fifteen feet. The sides of the rock are four or five yards asunder. Between these two sides runs, or rather falls, a rapid river ten or twelve feet deep, which, probably, by its violence, through a long succession of ages, has worn the aperture. About four yards below the summit of this cleft rock is a bridge of one arch, which covers the span, said to have been erected by the monks in 1087. A bridge placed so much below the road must have been inconvenient to the passengers; however, during that dull period of 666 years it could not be inconvenient to *many*.

As time, peace, population, and property increased, the evil was more felt; another bridge therefore was erected exactly over this in 1753. I descended the bank and entered upon the under bridge, standing upon one bridge and under the other, about six feet asunder.

The

The imprisoned river, having rapidly passed this narrow defile, expands, breaks with violence over the rocks, and falls in a variety of grand and beautiful cataracts. One of fifteen feet, another of eighteen, a third of sixty, a fourth of twenty, and a fifth said to be a hundred.

The derivation of the name may, perhaps, excite a smile: I shall give it from the tradition of the country, which, I believe, is credited by the lower class, for their faith is very capacious.

"An old woman, in search of her strayed
"cow, saw her on the opposite side of the
"cleft rock, and while lamenting that she
"could not come at her, the devil appeared,
"consoled her case, and told her he would
"accommodate her with a bridge over the
"chasm, if she would suffer him to take the
"*first* who went over it. As she *must* be
"ruined in one case, and could *but* be ruined
"in the other, she complied. A bridge in-
"stantly

" stantly arose. She debated a moment: her
" cow was dear—herself dearer; but the bar-
" gain could not be broken. She pulled a
" piece of bread out of her pocket, and threw
" it on the other side. Her dog, ignorant of
" the contract, darted over the bridge to seize
" it. He now became the forfeited prize. But
" as Satan kept no dogs but what had three
" heads, her's was of no use. He looked
" askew at being bit by an old woman, and
" who was more able to bite him? hung his
" tail and walked off." He behaved, however, with great honor, for he kept his word,
which is more than we often do.

Perhaps it acquired the name of *Devil's Bridge* from being what the modern beau would call " a devilish inconvenient one."

ABERISTWITH.

Pursuing our journey over a common of considerable eminence, I had, for the first time, a view of the sea, with the white waves incessantly

incessantly rising, and, on the right, one of the most charming rural prospects I ever beheld.

The town of Aberistwith is pleasing, like that of Langollon, at a distance, but viewed internally, it excites, like that, no emotion except disgust. The streets are narrow, dirty, and ill paved.

Perhaps the sea gains upon the land, for I was shewn a spot, now covered six or eight feet at high water, where, I was told, a church had stood, which is probably true, for I observed in the remainder of the steep bank, variety of human bones under sailing orders at a high flood. My eye was particularly attracted by a small double tooth, which stuck in the soil four feet below the surface, which I saw again in my next visit to Aberistwith.

The manners of a people are striking: passing four times through Wales I saw but one beggar, which was here. He accosted me, " Sir, I am a poor old man."—I was

struck

struck with the expressive manner in which he addressed me. Had this been in England I should have been pelted with half a dozen *God-sakes* and worthless blessings.

Strolling into a distant field, I saw about ten people of both sexes working together at harvest. They all stood still to eye me, as though I had been of a different species. I walked up and began a conversation; not a word was understood. Wishing to treat them, I pointed to them, and put my hand to my mouth, expressive of the act of drinking. They thought I was thirsty, and fetched their little keg to treat *me;* I frowned as a man misunderstood, pulled out a shilling, which I repeatedly offered. All seemed surprized, but nobody took it. I pointed to the pocket of one of the women to shew which way I meant it to pass; still nothing occurred but amazement. I now pointed to my own pocket, and then to hers, with the motion of giving; still the same. I then opened my

coat

coat pocket, accompanied with the act for her to do the same. This succeeding, I dropt in the money.

The dumb conversation ending we parted, all sides pleased. Had this happened in England, I should have experienced no trouble in *parting* with money, but instead of opening my own pocket, there were beggars enough who would have opened it for me.

Domestic affairs not allowing me to continue at Aberistwith, and there being only one chaise between that and Welch Pool, and that chaise twenty miles off, I determined to hire a horse and meet the stage at Shrewsbury, about eighty miles; but finding I must hire two, and a man, which would be still more expensive, and not being furnished with conveniencies for equestrian conveyance, I resolved to walk it, with my great coat over my arm.

A Welch tour is surprisingly grand. Nature is seen in extreme. The lofty, rough,

and

and barren mountains, opposed to the beautiful and fertile vallies, is a charming contrast. There appears no difference between the gentry of Wales and those of England, except that the former may have a little more pride, and a little more poverty; and the lower class, a little less knowledge, less poverty, and more hospitality.

MALLWYD.

In my first day's journey I passed through Machynlleth, a handsome open town, and on to Mallwyd, thirty-two miles; in my way, weary and heated, I stepped into a miserable hut; consisting of one small and black room, the floor native earth, and the sole light was admitted by the door, which had just admitted me. I sat down with all the freedom of an owner, gave a smile and a nod to the master, for to speak was needless. He looked pleasant, and without a word brought me a mess of buttermilk. This I could have relished, but was

too

too much heated. I afterwards, where I could be understood, mentioned this union of poverty and hospitality, the reply was, " That man is not so poor as you imagine."

In my second day's march from Mallwyd to Welch Pool, a man darted out of a house, as if watching for me, with a " How far are you going?" " To Canoffice." " So am I." I halted to observe a mill which I thought curious; he attended me as close as my shirt. He appeared rather shabby, not very active, but very inquisitive, without a wish to appear so; had travelled, been on board a ship, was a taylor, and was going to Llanvair to visit a son.

" You carry your coat upside down, you will lose the gold." " There is none to lose." " If there is none in those pockets, there is in others." We stopped at Canoffice, and, as I could make but a poor reckoning, I treated him.

The weather being hot, we agreed to repose in the shade. " Are your buckles silver?"
" Yes."

"Yes." We were reclined upon a bank, I facing him, unbuttoned, with my eyes closed, all in silence and abstracted from the world.

Opening my eyes, I saw, with astonishment, a large open clasp knife in his hand. " What do you do with that knife?" with some emotion. " Cut bread and cheese." " Why you have none to cut."

We marched on; I treated him coldly; he saw my suspicion. I was under no fear while my eyes were open and he not at my heels, for I could overcome two such, though no fighter. Determined to quit my companion, I out-walked him, which seemed to disappoint him.

Stopping at Llanvair to bait, he hunted me out, entered the same room where I sat alone, and drew his knife. " Pray why do you " draw that knife?" " I always carry it to " cut bread and chesse." " That must be a " mistake, for you had none to cut either " then or now, nor did you use it for any
" other

" other purpose. Besides, if you come to
" this town to visit your son, there can be no
" need to enter a public house." He closed
the knife and was silent. I paid my shot,
walked on to Welch Pool, and saw him no
more. I have only stated facts that another
may judge, but to this moment I am at a
loss to guess whether my suspicions were just.

LLANVAIR AND WELCH POOL.

Llanvair is romantic, has about fifty houses.
Pool is quite an English town, with about
four hundred. The streets are pleasant, but
the pavement vile.

Powis Castle is a splendid antique, with a
variety of curious paintings. The gardens in
the Nassau stile, now in disorder.

CHAP.

CHAP. II.

Mallwyd—Dinas Mouddy—The Yew—The Cottage—Head of two Rivers—Cader Idris—Dolgelly—Barmouth—The Welch Language—Eglwys Wrw—Bala—Pont y Glyn.

WE pursued the same route as before, till we arrived at Mallwyd, a little village in a vale, surrounded with mountains. Here is a considerable inn, where the tourist will meet with accommodations and civility. Here two romantic rivers unite; in one of them is a salmon leap, which produces the best salmon I ever tasted; the other rattles through a deep glen, fringed with wood.

DINAS MOUDDY.

I was given to understand, " that this place " held a considerable eminence in the scale " of Welch towns, was the property of the " ancient family of Mitton; that it was one

" of

"of the five lordships in Wales that were in-
"dependent manors, and exempted from tri-
"bute to the prince; that it held a govern-
"ment within itself, consisting of a mayor
"and aldermen, with all the magnificent
"insignia and ornamental trappings of a
"corporation." I had observed also, its name distinguished with bold letters in our maps.

I wished to visit this favored place, but my way did not lie through it. Being detained, however, at Mallwyd by the rain, and Dinas Mouddy distant only a mile and a half, I watched the opportunity of a fair gleam, left the company I had accidentally met at the inn, to their wine and their conversation, and stole a visit to this important place.

Enquiring my way at a cottage, there appeared about half a dozen young people, who, observing a dress different from their own, and hearing an English voice, which, perhaps, they never heard before, treated me wi with a horse laugh; a senior reprimanded them.

The situation of Dinas Mouddy is romantic, singular, and beautiful, upon a small flat made by nature and improved by art, on the declivity of a mountain prodigiously elevated, and nearly perpendicular, on the left descending to the town; and, on the right, continuing the same steep down to the river Dovy, which washes its foot. The road winds round the hill in the shape of a bow, and the houses take the same curve. It appears to the observer, a town suspended upon the side of a mountain. Curiosity led me to count the houses, which were forty-five. One of these, by far the best, is worth, at a fair rent, perhaps fifty shillings per annum. This, I concluded, must be the parsonage, for who would deny the best to the priest? but finding there was no church, I understood this mansion was dignified with "the hall." In most of the houses I perceived
the

the inhabitants could not injure themselves by falling down stairs.

Although in England I appeared like other men, yet at Dinas Mouddy I stood single. The people eyed me as a phenomenon, with countenances mixed with fear and enquiry. Perhaps they took me for an inspector of taxes; they could not take me for a window-peeper, for there were scarcely any to peep at, and the few I saw were in that shattered state as proved there was no glazier in the place. Many houses were totally without glass—perhaps the inhabitants, rather than starve a glazier, chose to starve themselves.

Ambition seems wholly excluded. The dress of the inhabitants is of that kind which never changes for ages. It is made to cover, not for show. That of the softer sex, I was told, is a flannel shift, but this I did not examine; a thin petticoat covered the lower part, and a short jacket the upper, both of woollen. I did not see the smallest degree smartness in the apparel, even of the young females. When a man chuses a wife, it must be more for the kernel than the shell.

I have reason to think their stile of living is as plain as their dress, for a swelling in front, from luxury, is rarely seen. One of the curiosities I saw, was a goat feeding, much at ease, upon the very ridge of a house! how he came there, or what he fed upon, I could not well examine, but only state the fact. Perhaps the people within, did not fare much better than the goat without, for I saw but one man with a prominence of belly, who, I learnt was an *alderman* and a *butcher*, and might have raised a front with the meat he could not sell; besides, we all know the idea of *alderman* carries in it something plump. The turnpike man, I was told, was mayor. Some days after, in travelling that way towards Dolgelly, I had a small dispute with Mr. Mayor, though we could not understand each other, for I found

the

the penny which passed current at one gate would not pass at the next. During my stay at Dinas Mouddy I did not utter one word, because I knew I could not be understood.

Returning, well pleased with my visit, I remarked to my landlord, a civil intelligent man, that I could not conceive the whole property of the united inhabitants of this celebrated town exceeded 600l. "I can tell "you to a trifle," says he, "for I know "every one of them well." After a short pause, he replied, "It does not exceed 240l!" If care attends multiplicity, these must be a happy people; their circumscribed stile of existence declares it. As I saw neither a beggar nor a person in rags, it corroborates the remark.

THE YEW.

While at Mallwyd the landlord took me to the church-yard to see a curious yew tree, from the root of which nine boles ascended,

that

that became trees themselves, each perhaps twenty feet high, and three in circumference. A numerous offspring from one fertile parent! They united in composing a beautiful head of 210 feet in circumference.

THE COTTAGE.

In my peregrinations about the neighbourhood I frequently entered a cottage, and began a conversation in an unknown tongue. I was struck with the situation of one, in a cliff, between two mountains, perhaps originally one, but worn asunder by a cataract; it was screened from all weathers but a southern sun. Upon entering it, I was surprised to find it inhabited by thirteen human beings, all in petticoats; I never beheld so much robust health in so small a compass, nor perhaps an assembly of any number, which produced so many rosy cheeks, fine skins, and regular features.

If

If I was not received with compliments, I was received with something preferable, *good nature*, which is true politeness. Not being sufficiently learned to talk to each other, we were obliged to converse by signs.

They immediately brought out the best of their provisions, bread and milk, which, though a favorite dish, I did not partake.

Their house, which was composed of a few rough stones from the quarry, and jostled together in none of the orders of architecture, consisted of three low rooms; one for the day, in which a small bit of turf was burning; one for the night, which held their whole stock of beds, and one for lumber, chiefly utensils for husbandry, all which they took some pleasure in shewing me.

The floors of all the rooms were native earth, and all nearly deprived of light.

I learnt that three generations stood before me, and though all in petticoats, two or three of the children were males. A fresh and
hand-

handsome elderly person was grandmother, three were her daughters, a fourth her son's wife, and eight were her children and grandchildren. They were all without shoes and stockings, except the ruddy senior and her daughter-in-law; their two husbands were employed in the field.

The covering of all the thirteen, though whole and clean, was supported at a small expence. They rented, I found, a farm of 100 acres at forty pounds a year.

The observer would be tempted to conclude this healthy, peaceable, recluse, and half naked family were without care, only, that he knows none are exempt.

I left this race of beauties with a smile upon each face, that smile which constitutes the major part of female charms, and which every woman should carry with her.

HEAD

HEAD OF TWO RIVERS.

In my description of Blackpool I made some remarks upon the use and abuse of *mile-stones*. In England they are in a disgraceful state, in Wales much worse: the generality of their roads are without them, and where they exist, they are of little use, being mostly obliterated. A small portion of care, without any additional expence, would make their utility perpetual.

From Mallwyd I directed my course towards Dolgelly, twelve miles. Riding up the banks of a river, I thought it curious to see it gradually diminish, perhaps for about seven miles, for, having no mile-stones, I could not ascertain the distance till I came to an elevated swamp, which was its fountainhead. But before I had proceeded many yards, I was still more surprised to find the same swamp was the head of another river which ran in an opposite direction. This I
followed

followed for fifteen miles. The first was a branch of the Dovy, which terminates in the sea at Aberdovy. The second, which increased as I pursued it, flows into the Onyon, and reaches the sea at Barmouth.

A similar instance of two rivers, the Clewidog and the Verney, may be seen upon Dolmayn, between Canoffice and Mallwyd. I have since observed this in various places.

CADER IDRIS.

Descending a hill of eminence which leads down to Dolgely, I had a full view, under a bright sun, of Cader Idris, one of the principal mountains in Wales. I attentively surveyed the top, and thought, if I was asked what length would be a line drawn from the eye to the summit? I should answer, "To the best of my judgment *one mile*." I believe the space is more than five; so fallacious is vision when it takes in only one object, and that elevated.

DOL-

DOLGELLY.

From the hill which I was now descending is a delightful view of a large valley, consisting of meadows, water, bridges, and the town in the centre, which had an agreeable effect, and all this surrounded with rocks, woods, and mountains. But when I entered the place, I found it was, like many of the Welch towns, only to be *viewed at a distance.* The streets were disgusting, and the pavement more so. The civility of the inhabitants, for I conversed with many, was preferable to the place conversed in.

BARMOUTH.

The approach to Barmouth (Abermaw) *was* over a prodigious mountain a few years ago, and might almost be said to have been inaccessible, for nothing but mere necessity could induce a visit from the traveller; and when there, he would equally dread a return.

return. I passed over this mountain from curiosity, but with the utmost dread, and could not conceive what should induce a people, except the apprehension of butchery, to place themselves, where, it might be fairly said, *they were out of the world.* They might *go* out, for fear of being *sent* out. The road is so very dangerous, that even the Welch keffil and his driver must meet with frequent accidents, and those liable to destruction.

The magistrates of the country, bent upon improvement, adopted a remedy, dangerous and expensive, though useful. The mountains of steep rock, jutting into the sea, they agreed with an undertaker to blow up, and form a road of a given dimension, above high water mark, and guard it with a wall, at two guineas a yard; which is now the most charming road I ever travelled.

THE

THE WELCH LANGUAGE.

Those things are often the most contended for which are the least worthy of contention; if they have no real value in themselves, we put an imaginary value upon them.

The workmen in the trades of Birmingham, whose earnings are of magnitude, have no trade-jealousy about them, but consider their occupations open to the stranger, while the stocking-makers of Nottingham, whose income is much inferior, exercise the most inveterate rancour against an intruder, and guard their trade as a treasure.

The Welch exercise the same kind of jealousy in an eminent degree. To a Welchman, every thing belonging to Wales carries in it the first excellence, and a little contradiction will give, what they call *the Welch fever*. I remarked to a neighbour of mine, that I was just returned from Llanidloes, his native place. " Are not the people remark-
" ably

"ably civil?" with an eye and a smile establishing the affirmative. I waved the answer—the question was repeated. I saw the little word *no* would have been dangerous, and was glad I had no occasion to use it.

Passing through a meadow in Anglesea, "This is a good piece of land." "Do you "think," says an ancient Briton, "there is a "better in all England?" I could have answered, "Ten thousand," but thought the words might as well lie still.

In conversing with many gentlemen upon the Welch language, a subject in which I was no way qualified to support an argument, I found, what rarely happens in England, they were all of one mind!

"Whether can ideas be more fully stated "in Welch or English?"—"In Welch."

"Which is the most concise?"—"The "Welch."

"As you understand both, which will ad-"mit the most flowers of rhetoric?"—"The "Welch."

"If

"If you should speak in public, which language would you chuse as the best adapted for the display of oratorial powers?"

"The Welch."

Our argument, I found, was not like a tide which runs two ways, but a river, which runs only one.

"I have frequently," I replied, "compared paragraphs in both languages, and generally found the number of Welch words exceed those of the English, which indicates prolixity. I have attended when a person spoke the same sentence in both, and drew the same conclusion. I have also remarked, when two people conversed, in Welch, the syllables issued like a flood, which seemed to overwhelm thought, and when they explained their ideas to me in English, it was done in fewer words."

"The Welch," it was rejoined, "is not only a language of itself, but independent and complete. It is expressive, copious, nervous,

"nervous, and flowing; but the English is
"*no* language, a mere non-descript, a medley,
"a Joseph's garment."

"But if we consult the Welch dictionary,
"we shall find one of the skirts, at least, of
"Joseph's coat, appertains to that tongue.
"Time and purity are incompatible."

This language, however, which was undoubtedly that of our forefathers, and the pride of Cambria, is in its wane. The gentry can speak it, but rarely do; even some of the clergy had rather omit it in the pulpit. The middle class practice both indiscriminately, but the lower ranks generally know none but the Welch: these keep no language pure. In public houses of every description, English is understood, and a few ages will probably wear out the Welch.

EGLWYS

EGLWYS WRW.

If the Welch tongue you know complete,
You then may ride, look big, and eat.

   Two learned words, when timely said,
Have sav'd a hand, a neck, a head;
But two *quite simple*, I can tell ye,
Have these surpass'd—*they fill'd the belly.*
   A priest in Anglesea, ill fed,
Preach'd a *whole* year for *half* his bread;
Sheer poverty, with dismal note,
Stuck closer to him than his coat—
For poverty was always nigh,
But his sole coat was apt to fly.
   Secretly pleas'd, he heard fame tell,
" A priest was dead—a living fell!"
His shirt and stock he bundled quick,
Slung them across his walking stick,
Then trampt it up to London swift,
(Lord Chancellor retain'd the gift)
Rapp'd at the knocker, shook his clothes,
And stamp'd the dust from off his shoes;
Though rather in debas'd condition,
Gave in his bow and his petition—

" Which

" Which begg'd his lordship would relieve him,
" And would *Eglwys Wrw* give him."
   Thurlow survey'd the words awhile,
With now an oath, and then a smile—
(Acknowledg'd his defect at last)
And for the first time was set fast.
" There are nine letters in this scrawl,
" Yet but one vowel 'mongst them all!
" Who can articulate to the ear
" When only consonants appear?
" Sir, you the living shall receive
" If you the English sounds can give."
   The parson bow'd again, and wrote,
Eyed, with regret, his thread-bare coat,
" The sounds, my Lord, for I tell you true,
" In English are *Egloois Ooroo*."
   " Who," says my Lord," " in black and white
" Can tell if he pronounces right?"
" Why Mr. Jones * can construe clear,
" Belonging to the Commons here."
   Jones wrote the words as soon as bid,
Exactly as the parson did.
   The priest the envy'd living got,
Then twice a week could boil the pot;

* I had the incident from Mr. Jones himself, at Barmouth.

In cotton gown could dress his wife,
And ride a *keffil* during life.

The Maw is here about three quarters of a mile wide.

Barmouth consists of about two hundred houses, chiefly in one irregular line, upon the flat sands of the sea, and under a rocky mountain. Part of the town stands upon the declivity of this mountain, forming eight tier of houses, one range above another, to which there is no approach but by steps cut in the rock. The floors of one row is about level with the chimnies immediately in its front; so that the first range regales the second with its smoke, the second the third, &c. till we arrive at the uppermost, which, in a westerly wind, takes a smell of all.

Many of these houses are rock, to which is added a little masonry. A spring of magnitude rushes down the mountain, which amply supplies with water every story of houses.

This place, recently in obscurity, abounds with inhabitants, chiefly methodists. I saw a boy raise his kite, which, in three minutes, drew a circle of twenty-nine children. From the plain stile of eating and wearing, the observer would suppose the people poor, which I believe is not the case. Œconomy seems to be the leading trait. A neighbouring attorney declared he could, at any time, in half a day, raise two thousand pounds in Barmouth. They carry on a considerable trade, and freight many vessels.

The traveller who visits, for pleasure, or sea bathing, is well accommodated, and is treated by Mrs. Lewis with every attention, and, at a moderate expence. *A wish to please* comprehends all we can desire. The company annually increases.

My horses did not fare quite so sumptuously. My directions were, " Never to see their ribs," but *here* I was treated with the irksome sight. It is, however, no wonder that

that provender is scarce, and bad, for the chief part of the country is rocky mountain. And what few farms there are, lie in a state of nature, which proves the farmer is not overstocked with labour. The women are more industrious than the men.

BALA.

We returned through this place, which is a pleasant one, and stands in a delightful country. The street, for there is but one, is spacious, but not the buildings. The pool (Llyn Tegid) is a fine sheet of water, three miles and a half long, and about three quarters broad in the widest part. This is the source of the famous river Dee.

The women are everlasting knitters of stockings; sitting, standing, or walking, the pins are in motion. We may fairly conclude, there is not an idle female in the place; nay, I have seen them employed while *riding*, but as the pins and the bridle demanded *three* hands, and they could muster but *two*, the horse was left to take his own course, which he seemed to understand as well as the rider.

In our way to Corwen we went four miles out of our road to see a curiosity, which we thought worth fourteen.

PONT Y GLYN;
Or Bridge over a deep Cliff.

This is a river which creeps silently along for some miles in an open bed, level with the meadows, when, passing this bridge, which is an arch sprung from each side of the rock, it falls with violence among the rocky fragments below, and, perhaps, in passing an horizontal space of fifty yards, sinks fifty below the surface of the earth.

CHAP. III.

REMARKS
IN
A TOUR TROUGH WALES,
In August, September, and October, 1797.

The Wrekin—Oswestry and Oswald—Llangollen—Owen Glendwr—Caractacus—Keniogie—Llanrwst—Conway—Aber—Rhiraidr Mowr—Way to find Sunday—Bangor—Virtues of Plumb Pudding—Caernarvon—Welch Wedding—The Jumpers—Journey from Birmingham.

THE WREKIN.

INCIDENTS beneath the notice of the general historian may attract the curious eye, excite enquiry, and give pleasure to the enquirer. They pay for research.

The want of health in my daughter induced me to take her to Caernarvon for air and sea bathing. But arriving at Hay-gate, eight miles beyond Shiffnal, she was too much indisposed to proceed, which gave me, what I had long wished for, an opportunity of seeing the Wrekin.

I ascended this famous hill, but the rain drove me back. I repeated the journey the next day, but the cold was intense. As a resolute examiner will not be disappointed by trifles, I ascended the third day, but the wind was too strong to command my step.

The prospect is not only extensive, but amazingly fine, for, the lands below, being rich and level, the observer looks down upon the beautiful inclosures as upon a map—the map of nature. Round the summit are the traces of a British camp, consisting of two trenches and two ramparts, one elevated thirty or forty yards above the other. Each of them encircle the crown of the hill, and each

each admits but of one entrance, narrow as a gate-way, with a small eminence on each side by way of portal. The lower or outward trench is more than a mile round, the inner much less.

This spacious camp would accommodate twenty thousand men, who would find it a cold birth, suited only to a hardy Briton.

I know of no historical fact that will attach to this camp; but as it is not certainly known upon what hill in Shropshire Caractacus, king of Wales, was encamped when forced by Ostorius, the Roman general, there is great probability of its being his.

OSWESTRY and OSWALD,
King of Northumberland.

Observing the figure of a man upon a stone pillar on each side a street, with a sword in his right hand, and palm in his left, indicating, I suppose, victory and peace; the same figure also represented upon the town hall; I was

I was led to enquire his name, and was answered, king Oswald, a famous christian, king, saint, and martyr, who fell in this place, then called Maserfield.

It appears that Oswald was a mighty benefactor to the church, and, in return, was canonized by the priest. But if we strip history of its disguise, we shall find him an elevated plunderer. How else can we account for his quitting his own dominions to ruin another's?

Penda, king of Mercia, of which Maserfield was part, being a Pagan, it was lawful, in those mild days of christianity, to destroy him and his people.

Oswald approached with his army to what is called the Church Field, then open. About four hundred yards west of the church is a small hill; here the battle began. The assailant seems to have driven Penda's forces to a close still nearer the town, called Cae Nef, and about the same distance from the hill.

Here

Here Oswald fell. Penda's people tore the body to pieces. The remains were interred by a spring about the midway between the hill and Cae Nef, called Oswald's Well, and a tree was planted on the spot; hence the name Oswald's Tree corrupted into Oswestry. A yew now stands upon the same place, which appears about two hundred years old.

His scull was found, in digging the pool just below the well, about the year 1780. In honor of the quondam saint, his head is carved upon one of the stones, banded with a royal fillet; and, though secured with iron rails, some rude hand has found means to deprive him of his nose. He fell August 1, 642, aged 38.

OLD OSWESTRY.

Remarking to a gentleman, that I had gleaned up some anecdotes relative to Oswald, he asked me, if I had seen Old Oswestry, where he assured me the town formerly stood?

stood? I, with a smile, answered in the negative. He told me, with a serious face, " that the town had travelled three quarters " of a mile, to the place where it had taken " up its present abode." This belief, I found, was adopted by all I conversed with.

At the above distance, west of the town, and two hundred yards on the traveller's left as he rides to Llangollen, he will observe a beautiful wood upon a hill. This is dignified with the name of Old Oswestry,

I could not pass this place without as strict an examination as could be expected from a man of seventy-four, who was to climb and descend a number of ramparts, each thirty or forty feet high, while up to the chin in brambles.

The whole is a considerable eminence, steep, and nearly square; had originally but one entrance, and that on the opposite side to the turnpike road. Its ancient name was Hen Dinas (Old Place) it is evidently a Roman Camp.

Camp, and in the highest perfection I ever saw one. When the traveller has passed over four trenches, and five mounds, which all round the fortifications are covered with timber and brush wood, he will find himself in an area at the crown of the hill, consisting of sixteen acres; where he may literally say, " He is got into a wood." The fortifications that surround him, I think, cannot be less than forty or fifty acres, exclusive of the area. The perfection of the works is entirely owing to the timber upon them.

When I had made my observations, I retreated to the possessor, to collect what traditionary knowledge I was able. He told me they had found something like a well in one place, where, he supposed, they hid their treasure; a pavement in another, which, he concluded, was to prevent the horses from injuring the ground; and pieces of iron, which, he supposed, were pieces of armour. That, about thirty years ago, as much timber

was

was cut down from the ramparts as sold for seventeen thousand pounds, which proves them to be extensive; that the proprietor could trace two falls prior to this, which must take up the compass of perhaps five hundred years; but how many before these, were hid in time.

It is not easy to determine what part of our history this magnificent work belongs to; but it is a work of immense labour, and ample security. It could not contain a great number of men, perhaps not more than a thousand; but, I think, it would employ five thousand men a whole year to construct the work. The people must have been stationary, and their safety consisted more in the strength of the fortifications than in their numbers. There are two or three out-posts. No battle, I apprehend, was fought here. I rather think the Romans constructed this laborious camp to awe the Welch.

LLANGOLLEN.

LLANGOLLEN.

A pleasant ride of twelve miles brought us to Llangollen, a small, narrow, crowded, inconvenient town, in a delightful country, with one good inn, and two miserable streets, in the form of a T. The church is elegant, the bridge spacious, but the river Dee delightful. It keeps up a perpetual quarrel with the rocks, over which it precipitates with violence.

Upon the borders of the town is Dinas Bran, an elevated and conical mountain, upon the summit of which are the ruins of a spacious castle.

A mile west, and the same distance from the town, is an Abbey, called the Vale of St. Crucis. For a recluse life, a spot more proper could scarcely be selected. It was built by Modoc, son of Griffin, prince of Powis, in the reign of Edward the First. Much of the building remains, and the whole may be traced.

OWEN

OWEN GLENDWR.

Sycharth (pronounced Sychyer) the name of a moat, once the residence of the famous Owen Glendwr, the greatest general Wales ever produced, the scourge of the English, a tormenting thorn to Henry the Fourth, and the ruin of his country. It must, however, be confessed, that Owen was an injured person; that he could not procure any redress for his wrongs but by the sword; and when necessity forces a man upon rough measures, he is not altogether responsible for the consequence.

In my tour through Wales I could not refrain interesting myself in this great man's affairs. I found the moat, where his palace stood, seven miles from Llangollen, and three short of Corwen. It joined the turnpike road till 1796, when the farmer inclosed a slice of waste land from the road, perhaps ten yards wide, which places it at that distance.

tance. It is surrounded with only one trench, which was deep, for the ground being elevated above the river Dee, which runs twenty yards behind it, a deep cut supplied the water from the river, which became an ample security.

The moat is nearly square, not a quarter of acre, which refutes what Owen's bard, Solo Goch, sung, " That his house was as large as " Westminster Hall;" this, also, Mr. Pennant might have refuted, had he surveyed the place. Not the least remains of the buildings are seen. There is a small swell near the centre, where the house stood.

Here Owen lived in all the splendor of his day, till urged to arms by ill treatment. In the same close, fifty yards nearer Cotwen, is an artificial mount thirty feet high, on which, within memory, stood an old oak, prior to that, a watch-tower, but now a clump of firs.

Owen usually attended divine service at Corwen church, where I was shewn a doorway, now made up, through which he entered to his pew in the chancel. Upon one of the stones is cut, half an inch deep, the figure of a dagger, and my guide told me, with a face more serious than my own " that " upon the Berwyn Mountain, behind the " church, was a place called Glendwr's Seat, " from which he threw his dagger, and made " the above impression upon the stone." If this had happened in our day, the whole bench of bishops would have united in pronouncing him a *Jacobin*. Exclusive of the improbability of the tale, my friend forgot that it refutes itself, for the mark of the dagger is upon the very door-way through which Owen passed, which probably was not built up in *his* day.

I climbed the mountain to what is called Owen's Seat, among the rocks, and concluded he must have been more agreeably employed

than

than in throwing his dagger, for the prospect is most charming. Here the rich and delightful vale of Corwen expands to view, with the Dee in the centre. Here Owen might view near forty square miles of his own land.

While he lived the life of a little sovereign in his own dominions, a quarrel arose between him and his neighbour, Lord Grey, of Ruthen Castle, twelve miles distant, now in ruins. Their lordships were contiguous, but Grey wishing to confine Owen within the bounds of the Dee, claimed the hills north of the river, at the back of Owen's house. This unjust seizure produced a suit—Owen won. But Henry the Fourth acceding to the crown, favoured the cause of Grey against his antagonist, and produced that quarrel which lasted many years, sacrificed a hundred thousand lives, destroyed property, burnt numberless habitations, excited that animosity which is not wholly extinguished, and drenched both nations in blood. Grey was

the

the most powerful in arms, Owen in stratagem. Grey was backed by the crown, Owen by his faithful Welch. Owen expecting a visit from Grey, drove a great number of stakes into the ground, and covered each with a cap and jacket, which Grey mistaking for an army in battalia, retreated. Wishing to take Grey in ambush, he caused the shoes of his horses to be reversed, with the calkins in front, to give the enemy an idea he was running away, which succeeding, Grey became his prisoner. The descendants of Grey were afterwards Dukes of Kent.

The same room is now in being at Machynlleth, low, gloomy, lined with stone walls, and a mud floor, wherein Owen held his parliament; and, where he took upon himself, with the consent of the states the sovereignty of Wales.

As the power of England was superior to that of Wales, Owen was crushed, and lived in retirement. Three of his daughters were married

married to three Herefordshire gentlemen, whose descendants are in high life, *Croft*, *Monnington*, and *Scudamore*. Owen died in 1415, at his daughter Monnington's, at the age of sixty, and was interred in that church yard.

I paid a visit to Rug, the seat of Colonel Salisbury, successor to Owen as Lord of Corwen, and saw a dagger, knife, and fork, all in one sheath, but each in a distinct apartment, richly ornamented with silver, which Owen usually carried. The knife and fork are rather slender. The dagger is about seventeen inches long, twelve of which constitute the blade, which tapers to a point. At the end of the handle is his arms, a lion rampant and three flowers-de-luce, curiously engraved. The principal part of the handle is inlaid with black and yellow wood, banded with silver; and the shield at the top of the blade, a solid piece of the same metal curiously wrought, but not much larger in circumference

cumference than a crown piece. The knife and fork are obliged to be sheathed first, which the shield covers, consequently the dagger must be drawn first.

Two observations occur from these remarks upon Owen Glendwr, that dreadful consequences may arise from a sovereign's offending even an individual; for, in this case, England suffered much, but Wales was so ruined that she has not recovered herself to this day. And, instead of the Welch crossing the dyke to murder their neighbours, let them continue to improve their roads, and the English will enrich them by their annual visits, to view the wonderful curiosities of that principality, for there is already, I am told, more than thirty thousand a year spent by the English mountain-hunters.

CARAC-

CARACTACUS.

Upon the same turnpike road, towards Llanrwst, ten miles beyond Corwen, and three short of Cernioge, is the pleasant village of Cerig y Druidian, the abode of the Druids, but nothing belonging to that domineering order of men is now seen.

Upon the first hill, east of this village, and distant one mile, is Pen Gweryn, where the Antiquary will be pleased with the small remains of a castle belonging to the celebrated Caractacus: the residence of a leading man in British history, but neglected by the historian.

As the traveller approaches the top of the hill, which is of easy ascent, he first comes to a trench about thirty-six feet wide. A small part of the soil having been thrown up on the outside, constitutes a mound three feet high, but the greater part being discharged on the inner side, forms a rampart about fifteen feet from the bottom of the trench. This rampart encircles the upper part of the hill, rather of an oval form, is every where visible, in some places nearly perfect, and incloses six or seven acres.

Ascending sixty or seventy feet more, he next meets with the foundation of the wall, about six feet thick, which forms the upper area, running regular with the trench below, and inclosing four or five acres. From the thickness of the wall, now level with the ground, we may reasonably conclude it ran twelve or fourteen feet high. As one part of the area is higher than the other, it points out the exact spot where the castle stood; nothing of which remains. The whole is a pasture.

The situation is on a considerable hill, but not a mountain. The prospects are extensive, but barren; and its affinity to Cerig y Druidian,

dian, proves that the prince and the priests were upon friendly terms.

We are told, that when this great man was routed by the Romans, whether at Caer Caradoc, Gair Ditches, or the Wrekin, is uncertain, that he retreated to this castle for safety, but was, with his whole family, betrayed to the enemy by queen Cartismunda, sent prisoner to Rome, where he delivered that famous speech mentioned by all our historians.

CERNIOGE.

Leaving Cerig y Druidian, a delightful road of three miles, brings us to Cernioge, a small and elevated village of three or four houses, but chiefly an inn of some magnitude.

LLANRWST.

LLANRWST.

Advancing five miles, we come to Gallt y Gwg, a terrace of more than two miles long, with the beautiful vale of Llanrwst forming a deep valley at our left elbow, and Conway in the centre. This, Burk pronounced " the most charming spot in Wales;" which I am more inclined to believe, than some things he asserted.

The bridge is famous, erected by Inigo Jones, but has a flimsy look. The town is low, the streets dirty, ill paved, and the people civil.

CONWAY.
(*ABERCONWAY.*)

Approaching this place, we were seized by the scouts of the innkeepers, at the entrance, for there is but one, who contended for us,

as

as Gabriel and Satan did for Moses. At that inn, which won us, we found neglect, and dirty sheets; at the other, every thing we wished, accompanied with civility.

In two points of view, Conway appears charming, that approaching from Llanrwst, where the castle, and the walls inclosing the town, appear in full majesty; but chiefly in that on the outside of the south wall, upon the sea bank, where the town, the turrets, and the castle, backed by a most beautiful and rising wood, has a surprising effect. This beauty is still augmented by a declining sun.

ABER.
(*RHAIADR MOAR.*)

Aber, nine miles from Conway, is a small and pleasant village in a Glen by the sea, once the habitation of Llewelin the Great. Here is a remarkable water-fall.

The

The Cataract is two hundred feet high, and more than two miles behind the village. It becomes a river of the same name. Some idea may be formed of the quantity of water which tumbles down this precipitous rock; I saw it in its highest perfection in the wet season of August, 1799, when the violent torrent washed down three bridges between that and the sea, all within the compass of three or four hundred yards. I saw it again in the extreme dry season of August, 1800, when the main springs were diminished, and the land springs dried up. The water, in this instance, kept Aber mill in motion, night and day, while the sources of the neighbouring mills were gone, and the inhabitants, for twenty miles, carried their corn to be ground at Aber. The flow of water in this dry season seemed to be about twice as much as was necessary for business. The fall from the rocks in 1799, looked amazingly grand; in 1800, beautiful. The issues in one must have been,

at

at least, one hundred times more than in the other.

One of the bridges washed down was that in the great post road to Ireland. The next, in the old road to Llanrwst; and the third, is what Pennant dignifies with the pompous name of "An Alpine bridge." When I read this sounding title, by my own fire side, in the best tourist Wales ever produced, something grand and beautiful strikes the mind. But travelling over it now, I found it consisted of two shabby poles, with slats nailed across, much like a miserable ladder, with broad staves, laid flat. The whole, workmanship included, cannot be worth ten shillings—A flourish upon nothing!

THE WAY TO FIND SUNDAY,

Without an Almanack.

That parson, who *two* trades sustains,
We must allow, has store of brains,
And yet his clerk, with only one,
Full twice as many brains may own;
But should you disbelieve me quite,
I'll place it in the truest light.
At Aber, upon Cambrian ground,
A sober clergyman was found,
This living held—'tis worth observing,
It's better name would be—*A starving*,
Which caused this union to be made
Of poverty, industry, trade.
Our priest*, for preaching had a passion,
E'er Almanacks came into fashion,
And, to miss Sunday, was afraid,
As no *red letter* came to aid;
But it appears, when wants are nigh,
A *genius* can those wants supply.

---

* He resided about a mile from the church, at the back of the village, among the mountains.

Among his poultry, one staunch *cock*
Told every morning " What's the clock?"
This useful point adjusted, then
Each *Sunday* was told by the *hen*;
Thus, must a priest be doubly bless'd,
Who two such worthy friends possess'd.

Miss hen was fertile, just like May,
And laid him one egg ev'ry day;
The thriving parson thought it best,
" That once a week he clear'd the nest,
" And if he counts the first from Monday,
" The seventh egg would shew him Sunday."
He never thought the week went round,
Till he the seventh egg had found;
And pray, what scheme could suit him better,
This egg became the Sunday letter,
Then gown and cassock, book and band,
With hat and rose, were brought to hand.

But who can property conceal,
When thieves are on the watch to steal;
The treacherous clerk had left his bed
(Forgot what in the desk he'd read
Fair written in his godly book)
Assail'd the nest, and one egg took.

Sunday, and people, now appear
At church, but ah! no priest was there,

The

The pious clerk ran back a mile,
The congregation waited while,
And here, I must divulge the news,
He found the parson *soleing shoes*;
Of priest, and people, we may say,
He *mended*, though *they* went astray,
If other souls were then forgot,
We must confess, his own were not.

" O Sir!" (in Welch) " a little sour,
The folks have waited full an hour."

" 'Tis Saturday," the priest express'd,
" Here's but six eggs within the nest!"
But we'll not stay to argue long,
He was convinc'd by Roger's tongue.

In horror, he kick'd o'er the stall,
Threw down his knife, and dropt his awl;
But as misfortune haste attends,
He quite forgot to cut the *ends*,
But drag'd them over hill and plain,
As horses drag the hateful chain.

Our heroes trudg'd apace—but mark
One luckless step made by the clerk,
Trod on the ends—the priest fell down,
Besmear'd his breeches, daub'd his gown;
He frown'd, he swore, turn'd back from church,
And left his hearers in the lurch.

During

During my stay at Aber, I attended divine service in this very church, and though I did not observe any pews lined with green, or the pulpit graced with crimson velvet, fringed with gold, yet I considered, that a man's devotion might be as sincere, and effective, although the walls were lined with green mould; a log of timber was his seat, and a wisp of straw, upon a mud floor, his footstool.

BANGOR.

When we alighted, I proceeded to the market place, to examine the interior of the city, but instead of finding one, I found myself at the other extremity, and was surprized at the difference between the grandeur of the name (City) and its size, which consisted only of one street, and 92 houses.

It lies in a dry, healthy, and pleasant spot. The bishop's palace is ancient, but neat, and in a warm valley. The cathedral is plain, as all places of worship ought. The church is large, with a short disproportioned steeple.

In the chancel we are treated with the melancholy sight of the busts of two decapitated bishops, a sacrilege committed by the rude populace in the destructive civil wars of Charles the First. These poor remains of departed greatness teach a more important lesson than ever they taught during their lives, that *" power abused, lays a foundation for incalculable mischiefs."* It requires some address to *arrive* at power, but much prudence to use it. Dreadful instances may be adduced from history of a mis-application of over-grown power, as that of the Romish clergy in the middle of the sixteenth century, whose abuse of power was borne till past bearing, and not being reformed, a whole system was overturned.

This was the case when the two figures alluded to, lost their heads by the furious populace.

pulace. The crown, supported by the superior clergy, carried an iron hand forty years, when the general cry, which never reforms, but destroys, rose against them.

This was also the case in France, which brought on the present troubles. Monarchy, aristocracy, and hierarchy, uniting to oppress, the multitude rose like a mighty whirlwind, and swept down all in one general ruin.

What great matters are done for the improvement of Bangor are, perhaps, done by the clergy, the Irish mails, and the stages, for it seems unable to do any thing for itself.

THE VIRTUES OF PLUMB-PUDDING.

Are you a Parson, bred compleat,
Yet scarcely know what 'tis to eat;
Should a Plumb-pudding hit your fancy,
Your happiness may ev'ry man see.

Examine Paul, for he'll observe,
" That he who preaches should not starve;"
Attend to what divines have spoken,
" This sacred text should not be broken."
The farmer's care supports his stock,
The bishop's is to nurse his flock,
Under the mitre, for their good,
Collects them, as the hen her brood.
I'll now to Bangor turn my face,
And there observe how matters pass;
Her churches I'll not write upon,
Nor streets, because there is but one;
Nor *ninety-two* compose my ditty,
Of houses, which compose the city;
My thought a nobler theme pursues,
The bishop shall attract the muse,
Whose blessing on his clergy lies,
They're taught to *eat*, and taught to *rise*.

My

My Lord (for I'll due praises give him)
Summon'd his clergy to dine with him;
That man, in harmony's a winner,
Who peace can purchase with a dinner.

   A hungry curate sat at bottom,
Who boil'd, and roast lov'd—had he got 'em,
For though his talents were respected,
Yet that of eating was neglected,
His work, what tailor good can call,
When he's no thread to work withal.

   On a plumb-pudding, full in view,
Our *curate* cast an eye or two;
His plate was fill'd, as authors tell,
All which he relish'd mighty well,
Nay, his lov'd plate was emptied twice,
Yet wanted still another slice.

   My Lord survey'd the scene awhile,
And scarcely could repress the smile:
" Sir, he call'd out, with some delight,
" You'll spoil both dish and appetite,
" Here's dainties, which are much more rare,
" I think will please you better far."

   With wishful eye, with shaking head,
And heaving breast, the curate said,

" This

" This is my fav'rite dish, my Lord,
" But, 'tis a dish I can't afford;"
He spoke as sympathy he'd draw,
The bishop *felt* as well as saw.

When a short season had pass'd o'er,
His Lordship summon'd him once more,
" What!—call'd again!—Who can endure it?
" He treats unkind, an *humble curate*,
" No horse have I—to walk on foot!
" Brings to the pulpit no repute;
" My thread-bare coat! Who can be seen in?
" Its black is transferr'd to my linen,
" And both, should an observer view,
" Approaching to one dusky hue;
" Tramp with an empty fob!—I must,
" Unless, my dear, you stow a crust."

Now, after bows, and after chat,
Just saying nought but this—and—that,
" Sir, says my Lord, there's in my hand,
" A *living*, much at your command,
" 'Twill place you perfectly at ease,
" And bring plumb-pudding when you please."

No lass, forsaken by her lover,
Could a more joyful face discover,
Should he return, and bring to view,
The wedding ring, and license too.

Whe

Who would not, to a brighter day,
Through a plumb-pudding eat his way!
A benefice, just to his wish,
Proceeding from his fav'rite dish.
The curate rose, by what he lov'd,
This was the spring by which he mov'd,
Held up his head—was more alive,
And taller grew, though thirty-five;
He's orthodox, most resolute,
Perfectly sound from head to foot;
Can, at his table, cut surloin,
Peruse the papers—drink his wine,
Plumb-pudding never has to seek,
He sees it smoak three times a week.

CAERNARVON.

The situation of the country which surrounds Caernarvon is remarkable, and merits the attention of the traveller. The whole Isle of Anglesea, twenty-four miles over, and seven miles in Caernarvonshire, east of the Menai, may be considered as one vast meadow, guarded by the sea on three sides, and by a range of rocky and majestic mountains on the south, forming a curve like a bow, the two extremities of which, Pen Maen Mawr, and the Rivals, project into the sea, and are distant from each other about thirty-five miles. Upon any of the eminences in the neighbourhood of Caernarvon, we have a compleat view of this beautiful meadow.

The observer, at one glance, may count thirty-one of these mountains, ranged in front; but how many thirty-ones compose the rear ranks is not easy to determine.

This

This natural barrier admits but of five narrow, and dangerous passes, guarded by five castles; Diganwy, at the opening of the Conway, which leads to Sychnant, at the foot of Pen Maen Mawr—Caer-rhun or Bwlch y Mau Fean, enters at Aber—Dol y Felen, at Nant Frankon, opens at Llandegai—Dol Badern, at Nant Berris—and Cedum, at Nant tal y Llyn, between Moel Elian and Mynneth Vawr.

This vast meadow, thus guarded, was thought the most secure retreat against the South, or stronger Britons, the Romans, Saxons, Danes, and Normans; and this, no doubt, induced the cautious Druids to fix their emporium in Anglesea, which is said to be a modern island, once joining the main land till the ravages of the sea destroyed the isthmus, near Bangor ferry.

Close within the range of mountains, mentioned above, runs a range of lesser mountains, forming a kind of lining, which still adds to the strength of the barrier. This guard

guard is farther strengthened by a line of about twelve forts, and these are placed the nearest together, where the grand fence was the least secure. Seven of these were pointed out to me.

Caernarvon is a handsome town. The streets are regular, though the buildings are not, and exceedingly well paved. It is the only place I have seen so in Wales; neither can any place be handsome that is not. The passenger should always be accommodated, whether he rides or walks, with an easy and safe passage. Most of the Welch towns have the two faults of narrow streets and bad pavement; faults not to be excused.

The parade between the castle and the sea, is beautiful, clean, convenient, and much frequented, but the Bangor turnpike road, which is delightful, is more, being unimpeded with dirt, dust, or sea winds.

I found the inhabitants much more civil than I had a right to expect, and though a

stranger,

stranger, was indulged with books, information, &c. and found myself happy among them.

Owing to various enquiries after druidical remains, in Anglesea, which I intended to visit, several gentlemen of Caernarvon offered to conduct me to the various places, and shewed me every attention; this I declined, as it would have led me to the tables of the gentry, and deprived me of a treasure I could ill spare, although I have received more than most men, *time*.

The savory dish and sparkling glass, were inadequate to liberty and my own plan. I had no doubt of meeting, in the island, with some intelligent person, who could speak English. But in this I was disappointed; I found the land in a low state of cultivation, the inhabitants thinly scattered, and the few I saw knew no language but their own.

An antiquary does not deserve the name who cannot fast half a day, and live hard the other

other half. When the guide was conducting me over Moel Elyan, between the lakes of Llanberris and Quethlyn, I held forth a piece of bread and cheese, and said, with a smile, " This is my dinner." " Thank ye," says he, supposing I had asked him to partake. I trust for drink till I meet with a spring, or an ale-house. The pursuit is entertainment for the head, not the appetite.

THE CASTLE.

When Edward the First, about five hundred and fifteen years ago, erected Caernarvon castle, it served the old city Segentum (Old Caernarvon) as St. Alban's served Verulum; drew it into its own vortex. Houses began to shelter themselves, for security, within the castle walls, which I apprehend is about five or six acres, and there are now one hundred and

and seventy-two houses, which compose nine streets.

As the powers of the castle failed, the houses increased *without* the walls, and there appears about six streets, and about three hundred houses more. All these are on the east side of the fortress, for the others are guarded by water.

The castle, at a distance, makes a grand and awful appearance, but within, like a man in a consumption, is drawing towards an end. I was curious to examine the room which gave birth to one of the most unfortunate sovereigns that ever existed; a title to an illustrious race of princes, and the means of uniting and making peace between two quarrelsome nations; that where Edward the Second was born. This I could only *see*, for no man has entered it, perhaps, for ages, having no floor, nor ceiling, but is open to the cellar and the sky. Upon expressing my disappointment, the guide told me he could take me to that
room

room in the other tower, which exactly matched it, and which I found to be thirty-three feet diameter. This fortunate, and unfortunate room, which gave birth to Edward, is in the Eagle Tower, and seems to an eye, without the castle, to be a chamber of considerable elevation, but *within* is a ground floor, because the land is much higher, and rises only three or four steps. It is nearly circular, or rather an octagon, is fifteen or twenty feet high, has *one* fire place, and seems, according to the fashion of the day, short of light, nor do the few, and small windows there are, appear ever to have been glazed, nor the walls wainscotted, painted, or white-washed, nor the least remains of tapestry or plaister! What would a queen of England, or the ladies of 1799, think of lying in among cold and bare walls? It would shock even the wife of a tailor, make a tinker's grumble, and that of a cobler strap her husband.

Three

Three roads proceed from Caernarvon, all excellent. On the south, that to Pullely, which communicates only with the peninsula, that stretches into the sea, about thirty miles, and lies between Traeth Mawr and the bay. On the east, that to Beddkelart, which is a beautiful ride; and a third, on the north, to Bangor, more beautiful.

The trade of this place, I should think, was considerable; for I saw one morning a fleet of twenty-two ships sail from the bay to pursue their several voyages.

A place of commerce, situated upon the sea, like that of Caernarvon, necessarily induces the inhabitants to venture upon that uncertain element, consequently upon melancholy accidents; but most of those accidents, which came to my knowledge, originated in imprudence. They excite both censure and pity.

Some time back, I believe about the year 1783, sixty-one people, men, women, and children,

children, who had come from Anglesea to Caernarvon fair, were about to return. It was ten o'clock of a dark and tempestuous night the tide was out, and the sand beds not easily discovered. Under these unfavourable circumstances, their friends intreated them to stay; but people, elevated with liquor, are not easily persuaded. They ventured, swerved from the usual pass, got about three miles to the south, near Abermenai, and struck against a sand bed. The most lamentable cries of distress were now extended, both to Anglesea and Caernarvon, but no vessel durst venture to their assistance. The tide was flowing in. What then must be the horror of their feelings, who saw inevitable death approaching by inches! Sixty of these persons perished, *one* only was saved, and he, by adhering to floatable matter. This multitude was lost through obstinacy.

While my family were at Caernarvon, in 1797, the man who guided the helm of the ferry

Ferry boat, in crossing to Anglesea, being intoxicated, fell overboard, and was lost.—He perished by the ale barrel.

A young attorney had come from Anglesea to transact business, which held him till a dark hour. He would not wait till morning, but, contrary to the advice of friends, the water being very low, would ride his horse over; I believe near Llanvair church. The horse found his way home, but his rider, the way to the bottom. A short time after, he was discovered, standing upright in the sand; his body, down to the waist, totally eaten away by some marine animal. His money was safe in the pocket.—Had the animal been possessed of fingers, his money would have gone first.

While musing in my chamber, over a book, in August, 1799, I was alarmed by a shrieking in the street. Looking out, I saw people running to the beach, in the utmost terror

terror. I followed, and found about a dozen people in great consternation, which, in three or four minutes, increased to five hundred. Upon enquiry, I was told, " a " boat had just sunk, with two men; that " they were bringing stone, had overloaded " the vessel, which striking against a sand " bank, and not yielding to the waves, " they flowed in, and instantly sunk her." One only could swim; the other laid hold of the plank, which bore him up. I saw their heads, like two small black spots, just above water, a considerable distance asunder, and more than half a mile from the shore. Seven boats issued from various parts of the beach, to give assistance. I saw them brought to land. They seemed a couple of sturdy fellows, advanced in years, who did not much regard their late situation. The most circumspect may fall, but he who voluntarily enters into evils, with his eyes open,

may

may meet with dreadful consequences; he who plays with danger may win destruction.

The market at Caernarvon is numerously attended with supplies for the town, the ensuing week. It is difficult to procure a joint, or even necessaries for family use, on any other day. Standing in a shop where provisions were sold, a person applied for some cheese. The mistress took up a piece which lay on the counter, nearly two pounds. How much do you chuse?" "The whole." "I cannot spare more than half a pound, for this is all there is in Caernarvon!"

The people of Anglesea are great supporters of the market, with the productions of the Island; and, I believe, often pinch themselves to supply others; for money must be had. The ferry boat, at Tal y Foel, is fully employed on Saturday morning and evening, to bring and return them. I saw it unload thirty-eight persons at one time, every one with

with a luggage for the market, and each solicitous to quit the vessel; and who does not rejoice to leave a prison? The men were assiduous, I observed, to assist the young women, but the old, who stood most in need of assistance, were left to shift for themselves. Some of these poor helpless things, in jumping on shore, jumped into the water, but instantly walked off, and a little ashamed; but I think the men ought rather to have taken shame to themselves. Perhaps the English fair are treated with more attention than the Welch. They are, however, treated with less labour.

Observing the sea very rough, and the wind strong, on a succeeding market day, I said to a gentleman, " Dare the people of " Anglesea venture over?" " Yes, but they " cannot return."

FUEL.

FUEL.

The first supply for the use of man is food. This must be had, for it admits of no substitute.

The second article of necessity is apparel. In a state of nature it is possible to exist without it, but not in civilized society. This, in a small degree, admits of a substitute, which is exercise. But the nature of man, not allowing a continual exertion, it can only be a partial relief from the cold. Hence the use of clothes becomes necessary.

The third principal want of man is fire. This he might also exist without, but it must be in a rude state. There is not an instance upon the globe, of a people, who could clothe, and were destitute of fire. Fire admits of no substitute but cloathing, and that in a small latitude.

Neither coal nor wood are in the neighbourhood of Caernarvon. Half this arises from

from the neglect of public good, and of the landlord's private interest, in not planting timber for beauty, profit, and use. Whoever visits Wales, sees her nakedness. British timber has been long declining, and there are two reasons why the generations of trees, like those of men, do not succeed each other. The landlord is too inattentive to plant, because no advantage can accrue in his life time; and the tenant will prevent the growth except he can make free with the crop. This neglect will soon become a national grievance.

The coal which supplies Caernarvon may be said to be purchased from the sea, for the carts run up to the axletree, to load foreign coal from the vessel. The inhabitants suffer great inconveniency when a supply is detained by contrary winds.—The remedy would be found in a coal wharf.

THE

THE WELCH WEDDING.
(September 13, 1799.)

My truth-telling Muse shall inform you what there is
Transacted upon the great Lake of Llanberris.
Exhibit a picture, in which will be found
A wedding—and life painted in the back ground.

'Mong the rocks of Llanberris, where foot comes not nigh,
No eye sees their summit except a bird's eye,
Nor ought in the prospect appears to the sight,
But water, and mountain, yet they give delight;
Quite silent for miles through these regions you go,
Except when the surly wind chuses to blow.
   But few are their neighbours, and fewer their quarrels,
And fewest of all are good liquors and barrels,
In stockings and shoes are no mighty sums spent,
In building, or gaming, or eating, or rent;
Instead of regaling in luxury there,
We see life sustain'd with the most simple fare;
Their health and their harmony are not disjointed,
For, as they expect not, they're not disappointed.
   Robust are the females, hard labour attends them,
With the fist they could knock down the man who
     offends them;

Here liv'd Peggy Evans, who saw ninety-two,
Could wrestle, row, fiddle, and hunt a fox too,
Could ring a sweet peal, as the neighbourhood tells,
That would charm your two ears—had there been any bell
Enjoy'd rosy health in a lodging of straw,
Commanded the saw-pit, and wielded the saw,
And though she's deposited where you can't find her,
I know she has left a few sisters behind her.

   A couple was led to the altar to join,
The youth fresh as morning, the maid five feet nine,
In her person, the best of all charms you might trace,
For innocent modesty shone in her face;
And in the beholder, 'twould cause a surprise,
Such a lass, from the lakes of Llanberris could rise;
Still, as I survey'd her again and again,
I sincerely applauded the choice of the swain,
Though on the priest's surplice no spot could I see,
I thought the young couple as spotless as he.

   All parties seem'd pleas'd when the fast knot was tied,
The parson, as well as the lover and bride,
For Plutus sway'd *one*, which I hold up to view,
While Venus, and Cupid, directed the *two*.

   Five miles, rather eastward, from Llanfair we go,
To dine with the bride and groom, at Cwm y Glo.

   Arriving, I crept through a hole call'd a door,
Some stones were laid down, and some not, on the floor;

The

The whole, a dark room, with three windows so small,
That the light down the chimney, quite outstript them all;
But this great relief came to soften their cares,
Neither sober nor drunk could they tumble down stairs.

Two beds grac'd the mansion, which made it appear,
That cleanliness, prudence, and order, reign'd there;
The tables, and cupboards, which opened to view,
Shew'd the hand of industry had polish'd their hue;
The shelves, and their crockery, both china and delph,
Were clean, and were decently rang'd on the shelf.

Dad, mam, and nine children, which fortune bestow'd,
In harmony liv'd in this darksome abode;
Nor can we consent to call those people poor,
Where prudence steps in, and bars want from the door.

A fire of square peat, and sufficiently dry'd,
Was spread on the hearth, and at least, four feet wide,
Over which, took their station, six kettles or more,
Which promis'd a feast—when they open'd their store;
And round this flat furnace, to keep them quite hot,
Were plac'd twelve more vessels, which held—God knows what;
Four cooks, in short bed-gowns, attend, by desire,
Like the witches in Macbeth, to stir up the fire.

Forty trenchers, with dull knives, and forks made no brighter,
Were spread on some napkins, which once had been whiter,

Supported

Supported by planks, forty feet long or more,
Compleatly were rang'd on the grass, out of door;
But here we are bound the word *table* to offer,
That our verses great dignity never may suffer,
The *table* prepar'd, and the cooking compleated,
'Twas perfectly needful the guests should be seated.

Loose boards were erected, on stones, with great art,
But proving too hard for a certain broad part,
A number of cushions were instantly made,
But not with a needle—No—form'd with a spade;
The finest of ling, root and branch, from the common
Par'd off, prov'd a cushion for both man and woman.

Now folks, male and female, came in by whole dozens,
Of neighbours, acquaintance, of friends, and of cousins;
Exciting surprize! from a region of rocks,
Such orderly people should issue, by flocks;
Black stockings, men's hats, and blue cloaks, all admire,
Which appear'd to be every female's attire.

They eyed one another, on me their eyes threw,
A singular stranger, whom nobody knew,
But like the Welch fashion, I met, in the end,
With all the civility wish'd by a friend.

While many a longing eye glanc'd at the board,
The word *dinner* sounded—acceptable word!
It drew, as the sun beams are drawn to a focus,
The magnet draws filings, Breslaw hocus pocus;
Five butts of boil'd beef, of a gigantic size,
On the board took their station, exciting surprise,
On these, close attended, as guards, rang'd for pleasure,
As many mash'd pease as would heap a strike measure,
With cabbage, a pyramid, much like a steeple,
All these were surrounded with thirty-eight people,
Salt, butter, bread, mustard, we'll let pass along
As quite insufficient to grace a gay song.

Man's born to misfortunes, while lodg'd here below,
Of this Job has testify'd, some years ago,
An able young female, my left, hedg'd up tight,
And another as buxom, supported the right,
When the board which we sat on, too feeble was found,
To support Wales and England—we fell to the ground!
But when from dame fortune a fall we sustain,
We're not much the worse, if we rise safe again.

The girls ne'er regarded their fall of a wafer,
And I was invited to one rather safer;
When lo, a smart shower, in the midst of our prey,
Came instant upon us, and drove us away,
While all our provisions, unguarded by man,
Were basted compleat, like a sop in the pan.

The moment arriving when dinner was o'er,
Our places were taken by thirty-eight more,
And then a third set, nearly equal to these,
Sat down to the cabbage, the beef, and the pease,
Besides about fifty, remaining behind,
Who stuck to the liquor, for none of them dined.
  If a man could speak Welch, he'd express his surprise,
And say, " Such a crowd must descend from the skies,"
For water, rock, common, can only be found,
With a few shabby cots, peeping just above ground,
But this mass of people, composing our shew,
Assembled five miles, at least, round Cwm y Glo.
  And now an old bason gap'd wide at each sinner,
As if it would say, " Pay a shilling for dinner."
  I see Mr. Carbuncle ready to think,
" A fig for your boil'd-butt, 'tis naught without drink;"
Have patience, dear Sir, you shall know all about it,
I'm certain I ne'er saw a wedding without it;
Eight strike of brown malt, which Caernarvon had seen,
And cost the bride's father two pounds and seventeen,
Was brew'd into drink that would make *one* man mad,
But given a second, would make his heart glad,
Each quart brought in sixpence, and that was done soon,
His *cot* was a public-house *one* afternoon.
  The glass moving round,—no—the *mug* I should say,
The lads and the lasses began to look gay,

To

To smile on each other, to toy, and to joke,
I was an observer, and not a word spoke.

 The bard, in a rapture, his harp handled soon,
And twang'd with his fingers, to try if in tune,
The people selected, and pairing began,
Each lass was indulg'd with the choice of her man,
Like Amazons, more than like fairies, were seen,
Full thirty gay couple, to dance on the green.
Joy held his firm station till morning was come,
Each swain had the pleasure to take his nymph home;
In such jovial ev'nings, the fire of love catches,
And what can tend more to bring forward fresh matches!
With the scene much delighted the muse took her flight,
And left the young pair to the joys of the night.

THE JUMPERS.

There is as much necessity to change a mode of religion as a coat; for both, by using, become feeble, and wear out; they may, with safety, be renewed by a skilful preacher, and an able tailor. Time will again wear both to rags, and call for another renewal.

Whenever a new religion is broached, or rather, the renovation of an old one, it gives umbrage to the world, but the philosopher will examine whether it is monstrous in *itself*, or only in his *own eye*. No people, in a free state, were more cruelly treated than the methodists, and yet they taught the original doctrines of their persecutors; as if the world would not suffer a new religion, nor preserve the purity of the old.

Time, however, induces the professors to bend a little to the world, and the world to them,

them, which promotes harmony; thus the quakers were as much abused as they are now venerated. Before we censure, we ought to be certain we are right, and the censured wrong.

Perhaps many of the people in Caernarvon, like those of every other place, are not attached to any society of religionists. The higher class cast an eye to the bottle, and the lower to the stroll. I attended prayers twice at the church, where the congregation, the first time, consisted of sixteen persons, and the second, of eighteen.

I also visited a dissenting meeting-house; it was crowded. But the most numerous society of worshippers, I believe, are the methodists. I saw two of these; both ran over with attendants.

I had heard many ridiculous things of a set of methodists, called jumpers, for all new religions are treated with ridicule, and exhibited

hibited in an erroneous light. These, by some, are deemed " mad;" by others, " traitors, who read Pain's works, have de- " signs against government, and ought to be " suppressed by the magistrate."

Being told, September 8, 1799, in the evening, they were at worship, I hastened to the chapel, and found the doors crowded without. Gaining a passage, I perceived myself in a spacious room with two galleries, crowded with about five hundred people; many, no doubt, like myself, were specta- tors only. There were not many pews, the great body of the hearers stood in the area, and with a devotional aspect, indicating all attention. The preacher possessed uncom- mon lungs.

After a few minutes, he delivered himself in short sentences, with the utmost vehe- mence, evidently designed to strike the pas- sions of his hearers. Ignorant of the Welch tongue, I could not understand them, but

was

was told, upon enquiry, they were ecstatic sentences, selected from scripture, chiefly the Psalms. At the end of one of these issued a small *hum* from the people; a second sentence increased it; a third, still more, &c. till, in the space of one minute, the crowd broke out into the most rapturous violence of voice and gesture. Every one seemed to adopt a sentence of his own, perhaps caught from the minister, and continued to vociferate it with all the exertion of which he was capable, and this in a kind of tune or cadence. One hundred different tunes, yelling from one hundred different voices, in a single room, must produce horror in the extreme. I never experienced sounds more discordant.

That person was the happiest who could exert the loudest; continue the longest, and jump the highest.

They performed in parties of from two to eight. Some times the two sexes joined, but generally

generally not. If one began to jump, another answered him, face to face; then a third, fourth, &c. forming a kind of ring.

As jumping is most violent exercise, they were obliged to desist, at intervals, but the body was kept in motion, something like what I have seen in dancing. The hands, head, and feet, were more employed, but the tongue never lay. The parson disappeared when he had raised his people to that pitch of enthusiasm he wanted.

I, who did not understand their words, but could only observe their gestures, and hear their sounds, could scarcely detach the idea of quarrelling, and was fearful, lest, by standing too near, they should jump upon my feet, or I give offence by impeding their rough devotions.

They were all decently dressed. The females were the most numerous. Some of both sexes, advanced in years, made but miserable jumpers. They seemed just as much intoxicated

intoxicated with exertion as they could have been with liquor; and, had a thirsty traveller passed by, he could not have been charged with impropriety had he stept in and called for a pint.

The scene continued near an hour. It gradually wore off, for nature must sink under violence. I could perceive a small degree of finesse, arising from pride, in a few of the worshippers, who chose to lie by till the rest were exhausted, and then begin with double energy.

We may reasonably imagine that excessive romping will discompose the dress. The men's, I observed, stood it better than the women's. I had been told, the latter often lost their petticoats. This may be true, but did not occur under my eye, if it had, the loser was too far gone to regard it.

When the performers had exerted themselves to the very last moment of their ability, so that they were unable even to stand, the husband, or friend, took charge of them with seeming pity, and, I observed, cast an eye round, to see if any of their garments were giving the slip. Caps, handkerchiefs, and aprons, were obliged, by the friend, to undergo a renovation,

Upon enquiry, I found these boisterous worshippers were people of very orderly life, and, I am inclined to think, they are no more conversant with Pain's writings, or the arts of government, than with algebra.

As every shoot of the grand tree which composes religion is supported by scripture, I make no doubt but this inoffensive race can bring unanswerable texts in support of theirs, though I had not the pleasure of conversing with any one of them. Their ecstacy seemed to proceed from a profusion of heavenly love, perhaps founded upon the words, " Rejoice in the Lord evermore, and again I say,

say, rejoice." If this sentence does not *command* jumping, it gives a latitude. The conduct of David is still more in point, "Who *danced* before the Lord with all his might." Nay, he proceeded one step further, he *leaped* before him, and in a dress too thin to be delicate.

I have since had an opportunity of perusing their articles of faith, which are consonant to those of the established church, are nearly the same as those of the presbyterians, independents, and baptists. Their rules of church government are excellent, and correspond with the best I know, the quakers. Their rough exercise in devotion is not mentioned.

The mind of man, like his fingers, retains an active principle. If he can find employment for neither, he becomes a burden to himself. Strength of body and of mind may be considered as tools by which we perform

the

the business of life. If we use them too little, they rust; if too much, they wear out. It follows, prudence lies in the medium.

Being locked up in my apartment, by the weather, at Caernarvon, in the exceeding wet season of August, 1799, gave rise to the following poem, which the reader is welcome to be pleased with, if he can. It has one requisite which some poems have not—*truth*.

A JOURNEY

A JOURNEY
From BIRMINGHAM to CAERNARVON,
AUGUST 11, 1799.

To JOHN NICHOLS, Esq.

We long'd for a ramble, and this was our plea,
That we might deposit our ills in the sea,
For he's but a blockhead who cannot produce,
To hide his true meaning, a feeble excuse;
The great trunk is sent forward, Miss knew how to stock it,
We took ten farewels, and some cash in the pocket,
And when the two Greys we were mounted upon,
'Twas Hutton and Co.—that is, Catherine and John.

E'er one mile pass'd over, the rain came to vex us,
But an oak stood our friend, that it might not perplex us,
Tow'rds Dudley, through Tipton, and Toll-end, we go,
Resembling exactly the regions below,
In fire, and in smoak, we're condemn'd to abide,
While a Crater, like Etna, lies close on each side,
Nay, the fire and the smoak, in the horse track, we meet,
For it burns up the road which lies under our feet.

And now Wolverhampton appears in full sight,
Our labour is o'er, we'll repose for the night,
The horses well knowing the Swan in that town,
" Your servant, good Sir"—we dismount,—and sit down.
" To Caernarvon, as usual, your steer, I suppose,"
Yes, madam, to keep down our wealth, and our woes,
If with best dishes treated—a smile in their train,
And charged by fair reason—who then can complain!

Now Tettenhall's fair village, expands to our view,
The most charming I ever beheld, except two,
For Hagley, and Aston on Trent, I aver,
To the beauties of Tettenhall, though great, I perfer.

If Shiffnal's a town which no beauty embellish'd,
Yet soon it appear'd, that the coffee we relish'd;
Now Oaken Gates rise, which make travellers mourn all,
Who justly suppose they are regions infernal.
They may think it is doomsday, and wish to retire,
With horror, they see the great world set on fire,
And all that occurs, while two long miles they tell,
Are noises most hideous, rank smoak, and ill smell,
Smoak dry'd are the people, you'd think as you go,
As if they belong'd to the people below;
At Hay-gate we rest, for our day's journey ends,
Honest Wilson receiv'd us as if we were friends.

The soft rising Wrekin I mounted once more,
Which often I mounted but two years before ;

Nor

Nor shall crowded Wellington rest in the lurch,
For again I attended her neat little church.

 The smooth flowing Severn round Shrewsbury moves,
Attending, like ivy, the oak which it loves,
And by its slow motion, it seems to declare,
A wish, that like ivy, its station was there;
As you, my dear friend, are antiquely inclin'd,
You'll see in the Abbey, a tomb to your mind,
A piece of dull stone, which, by all that appears,
Has slumber'd in silence for seven hundred years,
'Tis a hero, or rather, a rogue cut in stone,
As every man is, who takes more than his own;
Sir Roger Montgomery wielded the sword
For William the Norman, his cousin, and lord,
And winning at Hastings, it plac'd in his hands
An earldom, besides a whole country of lands.

 At Ness-cliff, a cottage stands under the hill,
Where you with good chear, and good nature may fill,
The landlady treats with the best in her power,
You think it abundant—she wishes 'twas more.

 Old Oswestry rises, we may if we please
Do just as we used to do—sleep at the Keys,
The town, inn, and country, the prospects, and wood,
Will all tend to please, can we wish for more good?

 Farewel now to England, where true friendship lies,
For seas just beneath us, rough winds, and wet skies,
But although the weather began to be frightful,
The roads, hills, and vallies, we found most delightful,
              We

We point to Llangollen, where the Dee and P— tries,
Which loudest, and longest, can make the most noise;
But this variation will quickly appear,
One *pleases*, the other will *wound* the chaste ear,
By want of attention, that's ever your due,
You're forc'd to divide a dull breakfast in two.

Now finding compleatly we're wet with sky fluid,
We march down twelve miles, and put up at the Druid;
Here's two ancient Britons, who ne'er were trepanners,
Because never tainted with South British manners,
Hearts pure as their sign, and you'd quickly discern,
They'd weather'd threescore, and yet *trick* had to learn,
We told them they'd plac'd there, and told them no lie,
" A house in our way, which we ne'er could pass by."

Through a road as delightful as you'd wish to ride,
And weather too cruel for man to abide,
We reach'd Cernioge, but in a sad plight,
And there we determin'd to rest for the night;
But what man, though wisdom should come to his aid,
Is sure to succeed in a plan, though well laid?
Dame Fortune may step in and give him a wound,
And his airy castle be brought to the ground.
A *judge* had possession, some moments before,
So I, and my people, were turn'd out of door;
In scenes where distress is, should pity preside,
'Twill tend to relieve us—but *this* was denied.

Though the night and the rain were advancing apace,
And both me and mine, in a terrible case,

         Yet

Yet on for Llanrwst we're obliged to depart,
With rain in the clothes, and with grief in the heart;
Though nothing we thought could exceed this bad weather,
Yet the rain, night, and tempest, increas'd all together;
But in our afflictions, this thought will remain,
Tho' the clouds should hang low, it will sunshine again.

 Eight miles were pass'd over, but not one with glee,
We'd a hill to descend, which was much more than three,
A brow with so steep and so angry a frown,
It frighten'd poor Catherine, she durst not ride down;
So the poor drowned horses, commanded by John,
With saddle and pillion, were bid to march on,
While Cath'rine and I trapes'd on foot to the town,
Like two water rats, which the dogs had run down,
But when night commences, what traveller sees,
If *one*, or if *two* folks, are up to the knees?
With additional burdens we feel incommoded,
Because all our garments with water were loaded,
And just like the penthouse plac'd over your door,
At all points discharges, retaining no more;
We borrow'd apparel, fast dropping the while,
At the Three Golden Eagles—'Twas lent with a smile,
Now Ducks came for supper, these moisten'd with sherry,
Then o'er our wet journey we made ourselves merry.

 We walk the town through, see what beauties are there,
But find none *within* it—excepting the fair;

But

But though there appears none, we ought not to flout it,
Look round it, you'll see nought but beauties about it!
 'Now a priest, with his gun, rode full trot through the place,
Had assum'd a drab coat, and laid by his black case,
His dogs, men, and horses, attended the while,
Who, clubbing their aid, made a sportsman in style;
Instead of his *people* engrossing his care,
His flock might be *straying*, while he clear'd the air,
Perhaps he would say, " though a sporting he went,
'Twas not as a *priest*, but a qualified *gent*."
I'll tell a short tale, which you'll think apropos,
A tale that was told half a cent'ry ago.
 Sir Thomas ——, a baronet, well knew his trade,
Being bless'd with court sunshine, a bishop was made,
While on a large courser, his lordship was borne,
Pursuing, with rapture, the hounds and the horn,
A worthy friend met him, they stopt in full chace,
" I wonder to find you, my lord, in this place,
" How can the gay sports of the field, which I see,
" And a function, like that of a bishop, agree?"
 " When I ride a hunting, in which I delight,
" I lay by the *bishop*, and hunt as the *knight*."
 " But pray, if it happens, the *knight* goes to ——,
" What becomes of the *bishop*? My lord, can you tell?"

The

The Conway, the morning, and we, rose together,
Again to encounter this singular weather,
The Conway look'd proud, but the morning betime,
Look'd rather too sulky to dignify rhime;
The mountains their wonderful cat'racts pour'd forth,
Which instantly turn'd to white atoms of froth,
Though *water*, the traveller's judgment may bilk,
And make him conclude, they are cat'racts of milk.

The castle of Conway with awe strikes the eye,
But who can behold it in rain, without joy?
'Tis noble without, but within rather scurvy,
For gunpowder quickly turn'd things topsy-turvy,
The pride of the sovereign, the dread of the boor,
Now stands as a cypher, and frightens no more;
The shore, wood, and prospects, delighted again,
Nay, every thing pleas'd us—excepting the rain,
Rous gladly receiv'd us, set wider his door,
He found us, and horses, the same as before.

At the Harp we're immur'd while two long days are spent,
Because the dull clouds had not done all they meant,
On the third day we mounted, and set out again,
Once more to encounter the wind and the rain.

At Aber, the torrents three bridges had dropt,
Which again put an end to our course, and we stopt—
To a tragical incident let us remove,
Of deception, and conquest, destruction, and love;

But

But why bring *four* evils to be our undoing,
When any one singly, a nation can ruin.
  At Aber resided a prince of high state,
His moat is yet standing, Llewelin the Great,
In his wars with the English, success was his doom,*
He took a knight prisoner, and kept him at home,
A friendship succeeded, companions they were,
Whatever the prince eat, the knight had a share;
The captive had beauty, the princess knew this,
She wish'd his embraces, he long'd for a kiss.
When sentiments harmonize, 'tis but a door,
Which quickly will open, and introduce more;
If a private connexion ensued, I profess,
I'll give no opinion, but leave you to guess.
  Although the prince wanted to have him in sight,
And the princess wish'd more to possess the dear knight,
Yet a ransom was sent, and the knight must return,
Though the prince should regret, and the lovers should
    mourn.
  Soon after they parted, some acts came to light,
Between the fair princess, and late captiv'd knight,
Llewelin, a letter determin'd to send,
To invite back to Aber his late worthy friend,
Arriving, the dungeon must hide him from day,
'Till a gallows was built in full view by the way,

    * At the Siege of Montgomery.

Where,

Where, on a small eminence, down in the dell,
Sixscore yards from the castle, I know the spot well,
The valiant knight suffered!—what heart would not move!
The victim of treach'ry, the victim of love.

While hanging, the prince to his lady apply'd,
Then on towards the window he took her aside,
And while a sarcastical smile you'd discover,
Ask'd, " what she would give for a sight of her lover?"

When we'd view'd with wonder the charming cascade,
The sore devastations the river had made,
Beheld a small field, where good barley had stood,
But three days before, now destroy'd by the flood.
Land, barley, and bridges, were quite swept away,
And they, with the pebbles, gone into the sea;
Seen *that* spot become, which before held the grain,
The bed of a river, and so will remain,
We saddled our horses, and with a light heart,
Arrived at Caernarvon,—here ends the first part.

Pennant tells us, from Dugdale, that the above knight was William de Breos, a potent baron, in the reign of Henry the Third. I examined the moat where Llewelin's castle stood; it is elevated about twenty-four feet, tapers,

tapers, and is about sixty diameter at the top. The vestiges of a moat and its feeder, from the river, are yet visible. Upon enquiring into tradition, at the foot of the Mound, the people gave me Llewelin's question, and the ladies answer, in Welch, nearly as stated by Pennant, which I am inclined to think was the production of the prince's bard. In English :—

"Lovely princess, says Llewelin,
"What will you give to see your Willim?"

"All Wales and England, and Llewelin,
"I'd give to see my dearest Willim."

Upon a mountain, about four miles south of Llewelin's castle, and in a field called Car Gwillim Dau, is an artificial cave, where William de Breos was interred.

This melancholy incident happened in 1229. Llewelin died in 1240. His son afterwards married de Breos's daughter.

The

The fair and frail princess was Joan Plantagenet, daughter of King John. Except in the misunderstanding, caused by the supposed amour with the unfortunate de Breos, she is said by my valuable friend Mr. Richard Lloyd, the poet and antiquary, of Beaumaris, to have lived upon friendly terms with her husband, was an amiable woman, interposed her good offices with her father King John, and effected peace between him and her husband, particularly when the latter was encamped upon a mountain, joining Ogwen Pool, called Carnedd Llewelin, from which he saw his country in ruins, and Bangor in flames, which John had kindled.

At her request, she was interred in the monastry of the Dominican Friars, at Llanfaes, near Beaumaris, and died in 1237. Llewelin erected a monument over her, where she lay at rest two hundred and ninety-three years, till Henry the Eighth, who may justly be said to have murdered the living, and sold the dead, disposed of this house to one of his courtiers, when the church was converted into a barn, which still remains. Joan was ejected out of her little tenement, her coffin of stone was placed in a small brook, and, for two hundred and fifty years, was occupied as a watering trough for the farmers' horses. Lord Bulkeley recently rescued it from its watery prison, and it now lies, upside down, at Baron Hill, near the hall, waiting his Lordship's orders.

The coffin is in tolerable perfection, has no bend, like the modern fashion, for the shoulders, but is broadest at the head, and gradually narrows down to the feet.

The length is	6 feet	6 inches
Breadth at the head	2	2
Ditto at the feet	1	11
Depth -	1	6

As the sides, ends, and bottom, are very thick (somewhere about four inches) the cavity will nearly ascertain the size of the princess, which was probably about five feet six or seven; sixteen inches over the shoulders, and nine deep, in the chest. Consequently she must have been a tall slender figure, and, no doubt, handsome.

CHAP. IV.

As in some of my tours I made Caernarvon my head quarters, took apartments, and stayed a month, it gave me an opportunity of visiting the adjacent curiosities, sometimes on horseback, but oftener on foot. I shall, while here, describe them as they occurred.

DINAS DINLLE,

Situated six miles south of Caernarvon, close to the sea, is generally supposed to have been a Roman fort. The stranger will have an idea of this fortification by figuring to himself an extensive flat upon the shore; about seventy acres of which is covered with a hill which gently rises from the east, and south, till it becomes twenty yards high, and

terminates

terminates in a precipice on the west, which is the sea, and the north, now a swamp, and which seems once to have been sea itself. Thus far is the work of nature. The work of art, is no more than making a large agger, or trench, round the highest part of this hill. The area at the top is about twelve acres, exclusive of the surrounding mounds, which are two; one on each side the trench, covering about six acres more.

The soil thrown out of the trench on each side forms the two mounds; the internal is much the largest. From the crown of one mound to that of the other, is about thirty yards. The trench is about six deep, but was originally deeper.

Towards the north of the area is a small circular rise, twenty yards diameter, with a hollow in the centre, upon which, I apprehend, stood a watch tower.

In this hollow, tradition says, a neighbouring shoe-maker found a number of coins, chiefly those of Alectus, became rich, bought houses, laid by the last, and turned gentleman. The hollow favours this tradition, for it seems deeper than the Romans would have occasion to make it, except for a well.

There is no mound next the sea; the place was secure without one; it could only be assailed on the east and south; both these seem weak. The entrance on the east, or land side, appears unnecessarily wide, and not easily defended. Mounds, trench, area, hill, and flat, are now a common sheep pasture.

Half the prospect, from this eminence. is sea, including the south of Anglesea, which, from this point, has not an agreeable aspect; but the east view, over the cultivated meadows, bounded by the Rivals, Gwern Goch, the Cader, Mynedd Vawr, Moel Elian, &c. is charming.

CHAP.

CHAP. V.

CLYNOG.

A Beautiful little village, ten miles south of Caernarvon, guarded by mountains, on three sides, and the sea on the fourth; shaded with a grove, upon an excellent turnpike road, and in the midway to Pwllheli. There are two inns, where civility and entertainment are purchased at an easy price. The church is exactly according to my idea of a place of worship, plain and neat. It is also the largest I have seen in North Wales, except Wrexham.

St. Beuno resided here; was an abbot, a man of riches, power, charity, and pride; for, this last produces three fourths of our benevolent actions. He erected the church, which is a proof of his wealth, liberality, and good taste. He also erected a grand mausoleum, called St. Beuno's chapel, for his own interment, which is a proof of his pride. This kind of pride, however, is rather excusable, because it attaches to nearly the whole of our species; even to Pope himself, notwithstanding his veil of modesty in the following lines:

> Thus, let me live, unseen, unknown,
> Thus unlamented let me die,
> Steal from the world, and not a stone
> Tell where I lie.

St. Beuno's chapel stands about six yards from the church, which, besides the great entrance, communicates with it through a little dark old passage called a vault. The chapel is a capacious room, unpaved, perhaps, sixty feet long, thirty wide, and forty high. The Saint was deposited in the centre, and the shattered remains of his tomb are yet seen.

His

His fame, as he foresaw, increased after death, and he soon began to work miracles, in healing the sick, and particularly the rickets in children. One hundred yards from the church, adjoining the turnpike road, is St. Beuno's well, eight feet square, inclosed with a wall, no doubt, erected by himself, eight feet high, uncovered, and each side about the same dimension, with an entrance from the road. The well itself is six feet square, the residue of the space is taken up with seats and conveniencies for dipping. The place is now exposed to ruin, and the vilest filth. The spring is suffered to grow up, and the water is not more than a foot deep. I could not perceive it spring up within, and the discharge without would not fill a tube half an inch diameter.

The process observed in the cure was dipping the patient in the well at evening, wrapping him in blankets, and letting him
remain

remain all night upon the Saint's tomb. Cures were performed, and perhaps Beuno got that credit which the well merited, for we all know that emersion in cold water is a sovereign remedy for the rickets.

The fact is frequent, which destroys the novelty, otherwise we should be surprized at the influence of credulity upon the uncultured mind. "If a person looks upon this "well, and *can* see the water spring, good ".luck will attend him; but if he *cannot*, "bad?" What then must become of the half blind! or even of me, whose eyes have been in wear seventy-seven years? However, the fact, in each case, may be true, for no man can look upon it without being attended with both good and bad luck.

Some ladies have drank at a favorite spring to *procure* conception; but the slippery damsels of the ten last centuries, have privately drank at St. Beuno's to *prevent* it.—Did the Saint foresee this annihilating quality?

The

The devotional spirit continued till about 1790, when Lord Newborough ordered the tomb to be opened. The workmen penetrated about a yard deep, but finding no Saint, desisted, and, by way of finishing the process, entered upon the more acceptable employment of getting drunk.

A small hollow is left in the ground, and the fragments of the tomb, once elevated above the floor, lie a confused heap upon it. Lord Newborough, it is said, promised to repair the defect, and the inhabitants seem to wish it, but that must rest till a stone can be cemented which is broken into twenty pieces.

In the chancel of the church, is St. Beuno's chest; a solid block of wood, or bole of a tree, four feet long, fifteen inches high, and fifteen wide, scoped into a hollow, with a lid to fit, and guarded with three locks, held by the parish officers. On the lid is a nick to receive

receive charity. It is opened once a year in favour of the poor.

St. Beuno lived in the seventh century. The church and chapel have been rebuilt since his time, and the passage or vault is the only remaining part erected by the Saint himself.

He was brother to St. Winifred, the Genius of the miracle-working *well* in Flintshire. She also lies interred in Clynog church, where her effigy, in stone, yet remains, mutilated like an Egyptian mummy, without head or arms.

CHAP.

CHAP. VI.

LLYNIEU NANLLE
AND
DRWS Y COED.

THE man who becomes an author, exhibits his own folly. Seeing a passage in Pennant, wherein he remarks, " that the compleatest " view of Snowdon is from Drws y Coed; " that from this place Wilson took his ex- " cellent drawing of that exalted mountain, " but that it lies so remote it is rarely visited " by the stranger."

I could not rest without a sight of this unfrequented spot, though it would cost me a walk of thirty miles.

I had appropriated August the 24th, 1800, for a visit into Anglesea, and applied to the
boatman

boatman to convey me over Tal y Foel. He promised at six, but forgot his word. Upon a second application, he extended the promise to nine; but, considering his nine might be ten, or perhaps eleven, which would trespass too far upon the day to visit Owen Tudor's premises, and Beaumaris, and, unwilling a fine day should be lost, I altered my plan, and set out to Dinas Dinlle, already described.

I then took a circuit to the left, five or six miles, over hungry and cold lands; I could scarcely tell whether cultivated or common, with very few inhabitants, and those as poor, hungry, and cold as the lands.

This brought me in view of two charming prospects, Llanllyfni, a village beautifully situated among meadows, bounded by mountains, in the road from Clynog to Beddkellart, also, in that from Cricceith to Caernarvon; and, the most majestic view of Snowdon, through a vista, eight miles long, formed by the Cader

on

on my right, and Mynedd Vawr on my left, to Drws y Coed. This vista exactly comprized Snowdon and his two sons, Cryb y Distyl on his right, and Cryb Goch on his left. During this long ramble, I could not take many steps without casting a glance upon the grand object before me.

Here, after three o'clock, I had seventeen miles to walk. I passed by the two celebrated Lakes of Nant Nanlle, in a romantic valley, near a mile each, divided by an isthmus, twenty yards wide. On the right, by the lakes, at the foot of the Cader, is a small old house, where Edward the First, delighted with the spot, frequently spent a fortnight.

I passed Drws y Coed, or, Door of the Wood, had nine miles to walk, after sun set, made it very late, and dark ere I reached Caernarvon, and was compleatly jaded.
Every

Every reader, who has not acted like me, will be apt to say, " He has exhibited his " own folly." I can only reply in *Irish*, " Every man has his hobby-horse, and I *ride* " mine while I *walk* on foot."

CHAP. VII.

Capel Cerig—Glyn Llugwy—Rhaiadr y Wenol—Bettws y Coed—The Conway—Festiniog—Cross Hour—Beddkelart—The Land—Water—The Goat—Old Caernarvon.

SHOULD we travel a road which gives us pleasure, if we travel it back again, it may *double* that pleasure; for the prospects, being reversed, become new.

In another of my tours, while at Caernarvon, I passed through Bangor, to

CAPEL CERIG,

Where is an excellent inn in a desert, and where I slept two nights. Here is a small decayed chapel, hence the name, Chapel among the Rocks. Lord Penrhyn, I am told, designs

signs to erect another, which will tend to improve the country.

I now enter Glyn Llugwy, from the river Llugwy, a vale five miles long, inclosed by a range of mountains on each hand. About the midway I came to the famous Rhaiadr y Wenol, a hill of rocks in the bed of the river, over which the water precipitates with the utmost violence. A sight of grandeur.

I arrive at Bettws y Coed, the Bead-house in the wood, and, at the banks of the Conway. The river runs transverse, in which the Llugwy is lost, and the romantic valley ends. A march to the right, up these banks is wonderful. The rocks and the river are at perpetual variance, as if contending which should most delight the traveller.

It is curious to see the bold and rapid river diminishing to a mere gutter, and expiring in a humble murmur, as we rise its elevated banks, and draw near the source.

Leaving these wonderful productions of nature at Pont Rhydlanvair, I was obliged to
travel

travel the next five miles through an old, blind, British road, so full of turnings, that, could I have proceeded in a strait line, half the steps would have covered it. This road, I concluded, must have been made by heads without brains. It brought me into the great Irish post road at Pentre Voelas.

From thence I passed through Cernioge, Cerig y Druidion, by Pont y Glyn, slept at the Druid, and passed through Bala; these are already mentioned. I then pursued my course over a dreary waste of eighteen miles, through ten of which there are but two solitary houses. This brought me to

FESTINIOG,

Twenty-three miles east of Caernarvon, where I slept; a charming spot, particularly if seen in calm weather, for the situation is bleak.

Here are two or three water-falls worth notice. I saw, in my landlady, what was once the figure of a fine woman, and a beauty; but now old, lame, wrinkled, decripid, sallow, and a skeleton! I asked her, " Whether she " was not the person celebrated by Lord " Lyttelton in his Tour?" She answered, with a modest diffidence, in the affirmative.— Alas, how fallen!

The vale of Festiniog is small, but pleasing. Descending the hill, which continues three miles, leading towards Caernarvon, brought me to Tan y Bwlch, the romantic seat of —— Oakley, Esq.

CROSS HOUR.

While Wales was governed by a multitude of princes, war, desolation, and blood, was the consequence. We are told, " A house " divided against itself cannot stand;" this will equally apply to a nation. Allow a common figure: " While two contend for a

" bone,

" bone, a third runs away with the prize." Some have thought " conquest disgraceful;" but this cannot be the case when the victor makes the conquered equal to himself. The man conversant in history will find conquest sometimes beneficial to the conquered.

Howel, king of North Wales, was a tyrant. He had two uncles, Iago, who married Helen, whom he, upon a trifling pretence, cast into prison; and Edwal Vychan, whom he murdered.—Constantine the Black (Cawellyn Dhe) the son of Iago, incensed at this treatment of his father and uncle, raised an army in 979, of Welch and Danes, invaded his cousin's dominions, and ravaged Anglesea.

Returning through Caernarvon, towards Festiniog, his mother Helen led the van, and he closed the rear. At the distance of eight miles, he had to pass a defile, bounded by two mountains, Mynidd Vawr on the right, upon which stood Castle Cedwm, and Moel Elyan on the left, which narrow passage Mr.

Pennant

Pennant justly calls one of the out-guards to the entrance of Snowdon. These are so near each other as to leave but a narrow road for the traveller, and a bare passage for the river, which runs from the lake Quethlin, at the foot of Snowdon. As Constantine was passing this defile, his cousin Howel, unperceived, let fly an arrow from the top of Castle Cedwm. " Are you wounded?" " Yes." " Then " you are a dead man, for the arrow was " poisoned."

The news of his death soon reached his mother Helen, in the van, ten miles distant, upon which she exclaimed, " This is a Cross " Hour." The side gate, at which she stood, still retains the name of Cross Hour.

For want of a guide post to direct the stranger, I lost my way, October 1, 1797, between Tan y Bwlch and Beddkelart. Supposing myself wrong, I made enquiries, but could not obtain an English answer. Instead of travelling by land, I found I was
going

going into the sea, at a place called Traeth Mawr. I was given to understand, that I might ride over this arm of the sea, provided I knew the way, and the tide would allow. But as I had never rode through that element, I was more inclined to procure a guide by land; when, after losing two hours time, travelling seven miles in vain, and being afterwards thrown into the night, he brought me into the turnpike road at Cross Hour.

After night commenced, I had to pass the other out-guard to the entrance of Snowdon, Pont Aber Glaslyn, perhaps the most singular pass in Wales.

The serenity of the night, the rising moon, the tremendous roar of the river, dashing through the rocks, the narrow road, which threatened to let me fall from the precipice into the water, and the perpendicular mountain on each hand, which almost united, and seemed to promise destruction, had an awful effect upon the mind, and I was not displeased when I arrived at Beddkelart, in my way to Caernarvon.

THE LAND.

The traveller would be induced to think Wales was composed of the most sterile and fertile lands in the universe, for barren rocks, and fruitful vallies, are the general mixture. But I beheld with regret that agriculture is yet but in its infancy. The rich vales are greatly neglected, and much of the mountains might easily be brought into cultivation. The same stile of husbandry we were in, three centuries ago, the Welch are now; with this only difference, their roads, which are a leading trait in improvement, excel ours.

WATER.

WATER.

The hills in the peak, and the mountains in Wales differ widely in the article of water. A man, perhaps, may travel ten miles without a spring, in the former; but not one in the latter; nothing is more plentiful. Water sometimes issues from the summit of a mountain; but oftener from the side.— Riding in violent rain between Beddkelart and Tan y Bwlch, eight miles, I could not pass so few as a thousand cascades, by the clouds and the mountains uniting their force; thus was I at once delighted and distressed. But I have, for half a day, wandered among the hills of the peak, and saw none.

THE GOAT.

This old, and once numerous inhabitant of Wales, like the language, is declining; and like that, will come to a period. This

kind

kind of wild sheep, or mountaineer, is rarely seen. I never had a view of more than three in company, except one evening, at Aber, about ten of them were quietly driven into a fold yard, the size of a house floor, for milking. The males are the picture of grandeur, the females, of innocence.

Observing a male, in a field, near Caernarvon, I was so struck with his dignified appearance that I could not pass on. I attempted an intimacy with this venerable sovereign of the place, but he resolved, that *distance* should lie between us. Before a week passed, I saw, with a melancholy eye, his skin hang at a shop window, for sale; I remarked to the master, he had destroyed a friend, and made a widow.

I am told, the landlords discourage the race, because they are injurious to the growth of timber, by nibbling the bark. But there seems to be very little timber to nibble at. I do

I do not recollect seeing a tree which demanded the name of *timber*, except in the parks of Lord Uxbridge, Lord Bulkeley, and Lord Penrhyn. The Welch have but little idea of hedges, and less of trees.

History tells us, that the face of the country, and particularly the mountains, were anciently covered with woods; and tradition informs us, that when Edward the First subjugated Wales, he ordered the woods to be destroyed, as being hiding places for his opposers.

We now arrive at

OLD CAERNARVON.

The ancient British name was Caer Segent, but latinized by the Romans into Segontium. This is the progenitor of the present Caernarvon, and lies from it one furlong, upon a charming eminence, hence the name, City upon a Hill. Its boundaries are visible

on

on every side; it is an oblong square, containing about seven acres. On three sides, part of the walls are standing, in one place, twelve or fourteen feet high, and on the fourth, the marks of the trench are compleat. A castle stood fifty yards distant, upon the river Seiont, the foundations I saw.

Though the city was British, yet, both the walls and the castle, I make no doubt, were of Roman construction. The road from Beddkelart crosses this ancient city, extending one hundred and sixty yards, bounded by a wall on each side. On a stone 18 inches by 15, in the centre of the south wall are cut in large characters, S. V. C. with some other letters which are obliterated. This stone was taken out of an old wall, in the city, 15 years ago, where it had been placed by a Roman hand, and fixed here to perpetuate the relic.

During

During the prosperity of this ancient city, its boundary, I was informed, extended into a field of two acres, which joins the old wall on one side, and Llanbeblig church on the other. Not the least building of any sort stands upon the seite of this once renowned city, the abode of princes; the whole is two fields of grass ground, or rather one, which the turnpike road divides. Hence cities die as well as men; all the difference is, an unequal term.

CHAP.

CHAP. VIII.

SNOWDON.

ALTHOUGH the beauties of Caernarvon, and its environs, delight the gentry, who visit for pleasure, health, air, or sea bathing, yet it is unfashionable not to visit the Lakes of Llanberris, but chiefly Snowdon. Though they lie together, they cannot be examined together, each demands a day.

This is the principal mountain in Wales, is nine miles from Caernarvon, and said to have been covered with timber, which I rather doubt, because the rocky soil, and exposed situation, is unfavorable to growth.

It is guarded by two passes, which are easily made inaccessible, Mynedd Vawr, and

and Pont Aber Glaslyn, about eight miles asunder.

Here we behold an assemblage of nature's wonderful and rougher productions; as if the sport of the evening, after the work of the day.

Here Owen Glendwr retreated from the vengeance of Henry the Fourth in 1401, after he had sacked the English marches, burnt the towns, and destroyed the people.

Long interested in this sovereign mountain, I consulted many authors, but they were too defective to form a judgment; I also conversed with many persons who had climbed it, but found them unintelligible, sometimes contradictory, and much given to the wonderful. I wished for an impartial judge, who would describe fairly, and cause *me* to see as *he* saw.

At Aberistwith, in 1787, they pretended to point it out, but I believe they knew no more of it than myself.

At

At Barmouth, in 1796, I was assured it was visible at a few miles distance. I walked fourteen, enquiring for Snowdon. No soul understood me, I had forgotten the word y Wyddfa.

In 1797, I rode twice over its foot, in hopes of a sight. It was covered to the root. Returning through Bangor, I had, for a few moments, a glance of its summit, at about twelve miles distance. It appeared amazingly grand. This quickened desire.

Residing a month at Caernarvon, in 1799, I thought a sight could not escape me, but as Pennant justly observes, " the days proper " for seeing are very rare." A fortnight elapsed, with weather too dreadful to visit any where. Disappointment still urged me.

Walking upon the shore, two miles from Caernarvon, I gained a glimpse of this emperor of the rocks.——August the 30th, I packed

packed up some provisions, for I thought a hungry journey was before me, hung my great coat over my arm, and set out at day break, *solus*, and on foot, to ascend Snowdon, and return, if able, at night. I was a total stranger to the task assigned; I might as well have attempted a miracle. Fortunately, it began to rain as soon as I entered the street, and crushed my quixotism.

September 1, I set off with an intention of walking to the Lakes of Llanberris, five miles; boating over them, five more; walking round the foot of Snowdon, keeping the mountain on the right, sleeping at Beddkelart, and mounting up, if the next morning was suitable.

Upon enquiry, when I had passed the great Lake, I found but one man who could speak English, and he would have five shillings to conduct me to Beddkelart, which he *said* was fifteen miles. But considering that I had

I had set out late in the day, had lost two hours in waiting for a boat, that fifteen miles was a long stretch, it drawing apace towards the evening, and that night prospects were of little avail, I altered my plan, and agreed to give a man, who could not speak English, half a crown to conduct me over the mountains into the road at the great Lake Quethlin, from whence I knew the way home.

As my honest guide did not understand the word *half crown*, I shewed him one, which, he offering to take, I withdrew my hand, lest I should be treated as I was treated in Herefordshire. Being lost, in the evening, I agreed with a person to conduct me to Laisters Church; but, when possessed of the money, he quitted his charge, and left me to find my way in the dark.

I now had Snowdon on the left all the way, but hid, like an eastern prince, while all the surrounding mountains were clear.

The

The next day, September 2, walking in the Isle of Anglesea, I had a view of its summit most of the way; and on the third, strolling over another part of the Island, had the same view, with the addition of a cloud of beautiful white foam pent in the interstices of the mountains, while all above was bare.

Being led on the fourth to the Kilgwyn Mountain, the Slate Quarries, and Lakes of Nant Nanlle, I, for the first time, gained a sight of this prince of mountains from bottom to top, distant five or six miles.

September the 6th, I ordered my horses at seven, and reached the guide's house, by the cascade, at the foot of Snowdon, by nine. He, my servant, and I, immediately began to ascend. The sun was not hid one moment during the whole day. I asked, " What " distance to the top?" " Nearly four " miles." I thought if I could divide the road into distinct parts, I should be the better able to guess at the distance.

I ascended about a mile, rather boggy, but easy to rise. Some of the land would make good pasture ground, at a small expence. I then crossed a fence, and was led half a mile, rising less, but more boggy. Next, a swamp about four hundred yards, which is the only level spot in the whole walk. I had now gone about a mile and three quarters, in a strait line, at the expence of one hour. A prodigious chasm in the mountain was on the right all the way, and the summit in view, which seemed at so small a distance, that a man might almost reach it with the cast of a stone. At the bottom of this chasm were three pools of considerable magnitude.

I now suddenly turn to the right, and keep a line in the form of a bow, with a quick rise for two miles, equal, on the average, to the rise of a moderate flight of stairs. The whole of this road is rough, but not equally so, with loose slates, large stones, and pointed rocks.

No

No path, neither did the guide seem to wish one, lest the road should be found by others.

Walking required that attention to the feet which prevented me from viewing an object without standing still. Though there was a gentle wind, yet the heat of the sun, reflecting from a vast inclined plain, elevated perhaps forty degrees, overcame me, the blood was in a ferment, a sickness and giddiness ensued, and I was obliged to recline perhaps twenty times. Neither did I find much relief, for I might be said to lie upon a burning mountain. I deposited myself under a small rock, the shade of which; with drawing up the limbs, covered me, and I found refreshment.

The mountain is replete with beautiful stones, of various colours, and fine texture, which I think would take a polish perhaps equal to those of the Peak; others resemble spar, with incrustations. I believe, too, there are singular herbs, but I am not skilled in botany.

botany. Had my friend, Dr. Withering, been there, he would have entertained me, as he did July 2, 1786, upon Sutton Coldfield, with their names and virtues.

Travelling a little more than a mile in this fourth or last division, I came to the Green Well, so called from the verdure of its borders caused by the stream, which my guide said, " ran the same round the whole year." The passage must be rapid in so steep a descent. The flow of water would fill a tube about the size of a man's arm. The water is exceedingly clear, cold, and well tasted. Here we opened our provisions, and tapped our brandy.

Within half a mile of the top the way became extremely steep and rugged. Here another chasm opens on the left, or opposite side of the mountain, perhaps three times as large as that mentioned above, horrid in the extreme, and here the traveller complains of the narrow and dangerous road, in which, if he he misses a step, destruction follows. But he is not bound to venture upon the precipice; the road is safe, and he may every where make choice of his step, for a space of half a mile in width, except within a few yards of the summit, and even there it cannot be less than twelve or fourteen feet wide.

In *ascending*, if a man falls, it must be upon his hands, which I did several times; if, in *descending*, upon his back, or rather, his right side, which I did once.

I now reached the summit, which is level, a circle of eight feet diameter, surrounded by a wall two feet high and one thick, composed of loose slate stones, the produce of the mountain; one of them, near falling, I adjusted. Here I put on my great coat, which the guide had carried, and I had carried his stick, which proved a useful stay.

We sat down in this elevated ring to consume the remainder of our store, for the guide had brought water from the well. My design

sign was, to stay at least one hour, but I found it too cold to be borne, therefore did not stay more than a quarter.

The guide, I thought, inadequate to his office. He made no observations, nor spoke but when spoken to, and *then* I could barely understand his English. He ought to have been master of the prospect, and, like a shewman, pointed out the various objects.

Such a day, though clear, is not the best for a comprehensive view, because the air, replete with sun beams, hinders vision; the best is, when the light clouds are high, and the sun is hid.——My situation was wonderful and indescribable. Here a man may fairly say, " He is got above the world." The mountain is said to be 1189 yards high.

Objects seemed diminished to the sight, four parts in five. The adjacent mountains seemed reduced to hills, except Cryb y Dystyl, which attempted to raise its proud, beautiful, and rival head.

The

The noble Lake Quethlyn, at the foot of Snowdon, a mile and a quarter long, and three quarters broad, appeared but little larger than a duck pool. The two Traeths, Mawr, and Bach, where, two years before, I was lost, appeared under my eye, and excited surprise that I could be lost in so diminitive a place.

I saw the whole of the road between the Lakes of Llanberris and that of Quethlyn, which I had walked five days before, and knew was five miles, but now did not appear to be half an hour's stretch. As Snowdon extends to both, the diameter of its base must be about the above measure.

The distance between the Lakes of Nant Nanlle and Snowdon, viewed two days before, appeared twice as far as now, viewed from Snowdon to the Lakes. Thus elevation reduces space.

A stone I had passed, in climbing the mountain, perhaps twenty feet high, and ten thick,

thick, was reduced to the size of a block that a man might seemingly lift. Not an habitation, tree, or bush of any kind, appeared in these desolate regions. All was wild and rude nature.

Below, the heads of four rivers appeared to issue from the mountain. On the north, the fountain which feeds the Lakes of Llanberris, five miles long, becomes the river Seiont, and ends in the sea at Caernarvon. On the south, another, which supplies the Lake Quethlyn, becomes the river Gwyrfai, and meets the sea three miles south of Caernarvon. A third, on the south-east side of the mountain, becomes the Colwyn; and north-east, the Glaslyn, which, uniting with the last at Beddkelart, terminate at Traeth Mawr.

My situation was a compound of wonder, grandeur, and terror. A stationary white cloud on the north horizon, prevented me from seeing Cumberland, Westmoreland, Scotland, and the Isle of Man. A line of sea
appeared

appeared from the north, stretching behind Anglesea, and far to the south, to the extent of perhaps two or three hundred miles; and on the back ground, I saw four of the Irish mountains. The most beautiful part of the prospect was Anglesea. It appeared almost under my feet, though twelve miles off, yet, so *plain* that a man might be induced to think he saw every inclosure, and so *minute*, that if one person owned the whole it would not be a vast estate.

Four mountains, Cryb y Dystyl, Cryb Coch, Llwddy yr Arran, and Clewdd Coch, which Pennant calls the Sons of Snowdon, and I confess they are sons of a monstrous size, though much inferior to their father, stand as buttresses, and seem to aid their ancient parent. We should almost think, at a glance, he stands in need of their support, from the decay of his strength by the two amazing chasms in his sides. He and his sons

sons unite in a friendly stile, as every family ought, and are abstracted from others; for round them appears a foss, and round that foss a circular range of mountains, as if, like faithful subjects, to guard the royal family. The diameter of this foss, I apprehend, is about eight miles; it is bounded by the Cader, Mynyth Vawr, the two Llyders, the two Glyders, &c. forming a circumference of more than thirty miles.

I was seriously told, and it was believed by the teller, " That a man, standing " in this elevated circle, might drop a stone " out of each hand, which, in one minute, " would be seven miles asunder." The truth is, one would fall down the great chasm, but the other would be impeded by the stones before it could arrive at the lesser; or, if it was possible to arrive at the bottom, the distance does not seem more than a mile.

The guide told me, " He had led his horse " up to the circle." This I believe possible,

for

for a Welch *keffel* will climb almost as well as his master.

A clergyman remarked, " That a man " *rode* his horse to the top, and round the " wall, on the outside." I took particular notice of this journey, which must have been nine yards, six of which a *madman might* ride, but on the other three, I could not conceive there was room for the foot.

Two gentlemen and a lady, in September, 1797, began to climb this famous mountain. The sun shone, the day was windy, and the clouds low. In rising, they were obliged to hold by each other for fear of being blown away, and were as wet with the rain as if dipt in the sea. In this dreadful state they reached the top. The lady, elated with success, though she could see nothing, pulled off her hat and cap, and huzzaed for joy. Returning, the wind took them both away. The guide told me he found the hat a year after, by a pool in the great chasm, and wore it himself.

CHAP. IX.

Dol Badern Castle—Llanberris—Bwlch y Gwyddil—Bwlch yr Eisteddfa—Roads—Nant Gwynan—Nant Frankon.

DOL BADERN CASTLE,

I THINK, is the only remaining one in all the narrow passes. It stands between the two lakes of Llanberris, and eight miles east of Caernarvon.

As it was impossible for an enemy to climb the chain of mountains, which are a guard to Caernarvonshire and Anglesea, and as there were five narrow passes, the Britons secured each with a castle: this was the central. We are apt to attach something magnificent to the word *castle*; but here the word and the idea cannot well coincide. It is only a round

round turret, fifteen yards diameter, twenty-five high, upon a small round elevated rock. The castle and the rock seem well adapted to each other. One of the bastions of Caernarvon castle is nearly the size of the whole of this. It could not accommodate more than fifteen men. The British race of kings acted upon a small scale, compared to the Norman.

LLANBERRIS.

If the traveller is disappointed in the castle, he will, from this road, be highly gratified with a sight of the beautiful vale of Llanberris, about two miles long, and half one broad, containing, perhaps, four hundred acres of meadow, totally inclosed with craggy mountains, which forbid the sun, and exhibit the perfection of solitude. The earth shewed me her finest verdure, but whether she *ripens* I did not wait to see. I could receive

ceive a breakfast, but no more English than a smile, and a tap on the shoulder, from my landlady, with " Dim Sasnaeg me, and dim " Cwmraig you."

BWLCH Y GWYDDYL.

Leaving this scene of enchantment, I instantly entered another, exactly the reverse. A Bwlch is a narrow gap between two mountains. I was struck with astonishment at *this* wonderful spot. He who has not seen it may suppose himself rising a steep mountain, nearly two miles long, meeting a rapid river, in the centre, but diminishing as we rise, and ending in nothing at the summit; with an immense rock on each hand all the way. From the frosts, the sun, and the rains, which, for ages, have operated upon these elevated mountains of rock, they have been shivering to pieces, and fragments of all sizes have covered

vered the valley, which is one hundred yards wide; so as to annoy the traveller, and choak the river. The traveller may now and then get a fall, as I did, and the spirited river, like a termagant, continues an everlasting uproar, because his course is impeded—the whole is chaos.

Amazement and contemplation fill the mind. Many of the stones may be traced to the spot from whence they fell. One, of a semi-circular form, and the size of a large cottage, directed my eye to its former habitation, about one hundred feet high. Another, about the same size, was broken, by the fall, into three pieces, whose jags would have united. A third, nearly of the shape of a brick, twenty yards long, six wide, and five thick, had fallen across another, which lay flat, and, by its own weight, was broken in two, five or six yards from the extremity. This large stone, lying hollow, imagination

has " converted it into a cromlech, then, the
" residence of an old woman, or rather, an
" old witch, and at last into that of a sheep
" pen."

BWLCH YR EISTEDDFA.

After travelling up this scene of wonder, this wreck of nature, sometimes up stone stairs, sometimes through water, but always upon rock, I arrived at the top, called, " The resting place," when all the prospect before me was the other side of the same hill, and as long, steep, and watery. One of the ranges of mountain turned to the right, which was Snowdon, and the other to the left, tending towards Capel Cerig. In front was a third range, which ran parallel to both, forming a triangle space at the bottom. All the three were marshalled in exact order as so many

many troops of horse, and were as formidable. This was barren, solitary, yet dignified nature. Not an habitation in all the prospect. Not a human being, shrub, or tree, to be seen. Even the birds seem to shun this secluded place, to seek their enemy—man, Here the foot treads not; the fruit grows not.

Unproductive, as this place appears, it is, no doubt, thought I, the freehold of somebody, but I could not estimate the fee simple at more than one shilling an acre. It is space without use—freehold without profit.

During two days, did I wander among these desolate mountains, travelled about thirty-five miles, yet only trod upon two estates.

I was curious to know the value of land in a desert. One farm, about three hundred acres, including a new erected inn, which could not cost so little as twelve hundred pounds, is let at three and sixpence an acre.

Another, two thousand four hundred acres, at sixty pounds per annum. A third, six hundred acres, at five pounds per annum, which is two-pence an acre!—And here I might pay a compliment to Lord Penrhyn, who is the proprietor of one of the estates, but *that* cannot be praise from me, to say, what all the country says; for every tongue, which I heard, was loud in his favour. His works speak in the most convincing language.

As the stubborn rocks, at the top of the surface, yielded no benefit for the use of man, he examined the bottom, which produces fullers earth, colours, slate, &c. These employ the workmen, and are exported for general good. Thus, public interest is grafted upon private.

ROADS.

ROADS.

Lord Penrhyn is also constructing excellent roads in the most barren part of the island; which is the first effort towards improving a country; and he will, no doubt, accommodate the traveller with one of the greatest benefits, which comes at the least expence, *mile stones*. The stranger is always glad to see one, because he sees a friend, who will not deceive him. They enliven a tedious journey, and are peaceable company in solitude. If he travels from necessity, we ought to soften his hardship; if for pleasure, to heighten it. Neither should the stranger be at any trouble to discover them. They ought, as far as circumstances will allow, to stand conspicuous; on the *same* side of the road, and be painted white. Allow me to transcribe a passage from my History of Blackpool.

" The

"The first step towards advancing the value of landed property is *good roads*. Our roads have, in no period, improved so much as in the reigns of George the Second and Third; and there is none in which land has advanced with equal rapidity. If roads are bad, the farmer can neither bring improvement nor carry off the produce. The *good* open his markets, and the *bad* shut them up. This is also the first step towards civilization. A connection with our species tends to humanize, to soften, and promote harmony. It introduces knowledge, for we are better informed of transactions one hundred miles off than our ancestors were of ten. In a commercial view, the advantages are immence.

"Mile stones are an acceptable amusement. Nothing should be denied the traveller which tends to alleviate the fatigue of his journey. Every man wishes to know

"know where he is; *mile stones* will inform
"him. He considers them a succession of
"intelligent comparisons. They ascertain
"the exact portion of his past, and future
"labour; but when obliterated, he meets
"with a dumb friend, who can give no in-
"telligence.

"I think, in most of our roads, there are
"either none, or they are defaced, hid in
"banks, hedges, or so far destroyed by the
"rude inhabitant, as to deny information.
"Though their construction is modern, they
"quickly assume the antique. I am ready
"to think they contain an attractive power,
"for every stone that should inform the in-
"quisitive traveller, invites one from the mis-
"chievous hand. Threatenings, rewards,
"and punishments, seldom avail; human
"nature will be human nature, in spite of
"resistance.

"As it is wiser to secure the house from
"being robbed than punish the robber, per-
"mit

"mit me, as a remedy, to state a little in-
"vention which I introduced when I con-
"ducted the Alcester road. It is only a
"plate of cast iron, half an inch thick, six-
"teen inches long, and eleven broad, with
"the letters raised, to shew the name of the
"town, and its distance. The ground black,
"and letters white. The plate is laid into a
"block of wood or stone, according to the
"produce of the country, and plugged fast,
"with holes left for that purpose.

"This simple, and cheap invention, will
"prevent an evil which the laws are unable
"to cure; will protect public benefit, which
"prudence cannot protect; it will stand the
"assaults of vengeance, the peltings of the
"school boy; and, painted once in three
"years, the efforts of time.

"The guide-post is also an excellent in-
"dex to find a town.

" The

" The foundries in Birmingham can pro-
" duce the plates above-mentioned to any
" direction."

To improve a desolate region, almost in a state of unfinished nature, Lord Penrhyn has recently taken a farm of three thousand acres, into his own hands, and his next step will be to drain it, which will teach the farmers what they never knew, *to improve their own lands.* This is adding real wealth to a country; a benefit incalculable. It is a conquest without blood. It will convey to his mind more pleasure than killing twenty men in the *field of honour*, and I shall enjoy the thought of being the last historian, who shall record, the rent of land was two-pence an acre!

The mountains are steril, the meadows starved. He will, in some degree, reduce the rocks, and lay dry the pastures; try what improvement can be procured either above or under the ground; whether any part of his

his stupendous mountains of rock will burn into lime, and whether coal can be found to burn it. Turn that into a blade of grass, which is now like the round spindling end of a rush; teach the earth to produce; divide this farm into five or six. Increase the population of a desert. Teach them happiness, by the arts of peace, and improve a barren estate of one thousand a year into twenty.

There are very few things unattainable by man. There are instances of setting bounds to the sea; guiding the course of rivers, and I have no doubt, but one day, a bridge will spring out of the waves of Bangor, which will facilitate conveyance, and improve Anglesea; why then may not the lesser rocks of Caernarvon be reduced where there is soil for growth.

In the lower ranks of life, the women go bare-foot, they card, spin, knit, conduct the house, or rather, the hut, get in coals, pile the

the turf, dig potatoes, travel by the side of a loaded horse to market. And the men, they do—they do—I know what they do *not* do—improve their Farms.—Perhaps this may, in some measure, be owing to a want of confidence in the honour of the landlord—Leases cure many evils.

NANT GWYNAN.

Having descended Bwlch yr Eisteddfa, or, the pass of the Irishmen; a set of plunderers in poverty, invading poverty, and bearing to the right, I passed by a grand cascade, or waterfall from Fynnon Las, a large pool in one of the chasms in Snowdon. The fall seems about three hundred feet high, and the water, a bold flow. This forms the river Glaslyn, and brought me in view of the beautiful vale of Nant Gwynan; a rich spot, graced with woods, and with two pools of magnitude.
The

The whole, perhaps, two thousand acres, surrounded with dreary mountains; a diamond illustrated with black shades.

NANT FRANKON.

There is a pleasure in ruminating upon the beauties of Wales: as, the facility in travelling those roads which are improved; the prospects upon eminences; such as the sea, the lakes, the cultivated lands below, barren deserts, the grandeur of the mountains, the amazing prospect from Snowdon, the singular situation of Llanberris, the terrific chaos of Bwlch y Gwyddyl; also the beauties of the Nants, or vallies, enhanced by surrounding desolation. Among the last is that of Nant Frankon.

A stranger to the country, to the language, and almost to man, I returned from Nant Gwynan, slept at Capel Cerig, and was
wandering

wandering over Lord Penrhyn's new road, towards Caernarvon, my present home. The cascades on my left, were rolling down with violence, after heavy rain, when a sheet of water, a mile long, and three quarters wide, presented itself to view, which, by the map, I knew must be Ogwen Pool. But what was my surprize, when, at the extremity of the pool, I instantly found myself upon a precipice two hundred feet high, and burst, in a moment, upon a most beautiful valley, nearly one mile wide and four long; the river rushing down this precipice in several stages, and winding, full in view, through this delightful valley. The rocks were tremendous, the mountains sloping, and the verdure increasing with the descent, to the bottom, where, if poetically inclined, I might say, " Nature " sat in majesty, adorned in her best robe of " green velvet."

When

When I had travelled about three miles along this sequestered valley, I saw four people contriving how to mend a gate. I singled out one, whom I had no doubt understood English, nay, I could almost have told it from the very cut of his coat. I asked several questions regarding the road, and the objects before me; all which he readily answered; for being dressed in black, I might be taken for a clergyman, which is an excellent passport for a stranger. "My way, I "am informed, Sir, lies through Nant Fran- "kon, pray how shall I know when I am in "it?" "You are in it now."

CHAP.

CHAP. X.

ANGLESEA.

The Ferries—Druidical Remains—Bryn Gwyn—Astronomer's Stone—Tre'r Drwr Bach—Tre'r Dryw—Tan Ben y Cefn—Llanidan—The Carnedd—The Cromlech—Owen Tudor—Beaumaris.

DURING my repeated visits to Caernarvon, I frequently set my foot in Anglesea, was always pleased with the excursion, though I lost much by my ignorance of the language. I shall comprize my remarks, to avoid confusion, in one tour.

THE FERRIES.

Five Ferries, in the compass of twelve or fourteen miles, communicate with this island.

The most southern is Abermenai.

Three miles north of this is that of Caernarvon (Tal y Foel.)

Four miles still north, is Moel y Don (The Hill in the Waves.)

Three miles beyond this is Bangor (Porthathwy.) The narrowest part of the Menai, not half a mile wide.

The fifth, at Beaumaris, four miles over—I have passed at the three central.

DRUIDICAL REMAINS.

The remotest stile of action and character, that history or tradition can trace, of the inhabitants of this island, is that of the ancient Britons, our rude forefathers. The monuments they left us tend to illustrate both. Very few of these monuments are found in England; population and cultivation are destructive to antiquity. More are found in Wales, and still more in Anglesea.

During

During my stay at Caernarvon, I made many enquiries, and many trips into the island, to follow the footsteps of its old inhabitants, and particularly the Druids. I determined to spend two whole days in one line of research, and set out, with my servant, September 3, 1799.

I entered the common ferry boat, with about forty passengers, not one could speak English. Surprised to see every person carry a luggage, for family use, as bread, cloth, shoes, brushes, flour, &c. I was given to understand " they were obliged to cross the
" water for a supply, nor could they eat a
" breakfast till they had fetched it from
" Caernarvon, though some of them resided
" at the distance of six or seven miles. That
" it was the practice of the Anglesea farmer
" to sell his wheat in autumn to the Liverpool
" merchant, and, prior to another crop, often
" purchase it again at an advanced price,"

This Ferry (Tal y Foel) I was assured was three miles over. I believe it much less. But we are sure to meet with the wonderful in Wales. The boat, as near as I could guess, went at the rate of three miles an hour. The voyage was exactly thirty minutes.

My intended route did not lie more than two miles from the shore. Upon application to Evan Floyd, Esq. of Maes Purth, to favour me with a conductor, he observed, " he had " none who could speak English," *but* kindly ordered his boy to guide me to *Bryn Gwyn*. Whether he could speak Welch I know not, for he did not utter a word in any language, during his stay.

BRYN GWYN.

Now I seem to enter classic ground, where those objects of antiquity open, beyond which British history cannot penetrate. Here was

the

the Court of Justice for civil and religious purposes. Rowland, who wrote the history of Anglesea, a century ago, proves the words Bryn Gwyn to mean supreme, or royal court.

Here too, was a principal place of worship, being in the vicinity of the Arch Druid's palace. Their church was a circle of upright stones, whose diameter is fifty-two yards. But the ignorant country people, supposing money was hid under them, recently tore them up, which destroyed, perhaps, the the oldest cathedral in Europe. I am sorry Mr. Floyd, the proprietor, suffered it; but what we see daily excites no attention. Some of them are scattered; two stones stand about 20 yards east of the circle, and are four yards asunder. One of them, which is twelve feet by seven, exclusive of what remains in the earth, stands upright, and forms exactly the gable end of the house, for I saw but one in Bryn Gwyn. The other, nearly the same size, is also erect, and forms a fence for the garden. The house and garden were made to the stones. By what power they could rear up these ponderous masses, I did not enquire, because I could not receive a word of English; and if I could, they were unable to inform me. The stones of the temple are four feet high, and, perhaps, three square. I was now about two miles from the Menai, and one north of the road which leads from the Ferry to Newborough.

ASTRONOMER's STONE.

About four hundred yards west is an accessible rock 5 yards high, by the river Breint (Chief, or Royal River) which is called the Astronomer's Stone, but why the learned, in *that* day, should take their observations in a valley, I leave to the learned in *this*. The

reader

reader must understand that this royal river, which makes so conspicuous a figure in history, is a gutter that a man might skip over, nay, which I myself could skip over, if pursued by any animal with horns, from a goat to a man.

TRE'R DRWR BACH.

About four hundred yards north of Bryn Gwyn, is Tre'r Drwr Bach (castle of the lesser Druid.) This is not half an acre, scooped a little hollow, now a meadow, was the habitation of the inferior Druid, who, perhaps, superintended the service of the church, for we may fairly suppose the Arch Druid too ill, or too indolent to attend in person. His business was more with the fleece than the flock.

This spot is surrounded with a bank twenty feet broad in the base, and twelve high,

high, composed of stones, like those of the Carnedd, and earth, promiscuously mixed.

There are no traces of a foss, though there must have been one, nor the remains of a building. The mound is in tolerable perfection.

Two articles of dress, unalterably marked the Druid, a white surplice, and a large beard.

Many authors have treated on the *variations* of fashion, but I know none who have treated upon its *stability*. The Druidical surplice has descended, from one generation to another, without alteration, till it has reached the present time, so that the clergy carry daily the most antique fashion, in dress, we know; nor can we expect *that* fashion to change which is ardently coveted, and which carries with it a freehold title to power and profit.

The *beard*, which is no other than hair upon the head, has varied in appearance, but not in in use. The ancient Druid wore *his* upon the fore part of his head, the chin; the Divine, in our day, on the back, or, contrary part of his, vulgarly called a *wig*. The use of both was to inspire reverence in the observer, and pride in the wearer, who thought it of the utmost importance. Both grew to an enormous size, and were attended with the same powers and effects.

No Druid of ancient days, or preacher of ours, could make a figure without a bush upon one side or the other of his head. The wisdom of both, consisted in the quantity of this hairy covering. The talents within were measured by the bulk, and order, without. The correctness of the hair, and the language, coincided together. The beard was adjusted, and the wig was dressed with the utmost nicety. If a hair stood disordered in the ranks, it must have disordered a word; a lock would have spoiled a sentence, and a strong wind

wind ruined a sermon. Thus, quantity and order, was the sum of eloquence.

As the modern wig exceeded in bulk the ancient beard—so the eloquence of the latter was surpassed by the wig.

The gentlemen of the long robe, adopting the fashion, quickly surpassed the clergy in bulk of wig, consequently the eloquence of the bar exceeded that of the pulpit.

One small evil, however, attended the ancient Druid and the modern Divine; as neither of them could, under the pending load, move the head without the body, so neither could nod an emphasis to a sentence. But this was not altogether the case with the lawyer, for, possessing more energy, he would rather ruffle his wig than injure his argument.

TRE'R

TRE'R DRYW.

About the same distance, still north, down in a perfect swamp, is Tre'r Dryw (Druids town, if a place will bear the name of a town without a house) in which is an encampment called Caer-leb. Here was the palace of the Arch Druid. The whole is about seven acres, with several entrenchments one within another, all in a square form, in crossing which, I first approached a foss, four feet wide, which a man might easily step over, joining a mound of the same width—both had been larger. Then follows a plain of seventeen yards, which brought me to a trench of five yards; this my servant skipt over, but I, having lost the activity of youth, skipt in. Then followed a bank of the same dimensions, and both in a bolder stile. Immediately another foss of seven yards, and a bank of the

the same dimensions, for a moment impeded our progress, and both more elevated. All the ditches have been much deeper, and are now replete with water up to the calf. The banks are four feet high.

I now arrived at the centre, a plain flat of one acre, rather elevated, and perfectly dry.

On this spot stood the Arch Druid's palace, which inclosed the united powers of St. James's and Lambeth. Not the least traces of any building remain. Here we contemplate, with a sigh, the grandest spot of the British church, now a silent bog, unpassable, disregarded by man, and unprofitable to the owner.

On the farther side of the fortification is only one bank, which is eight yards over, and one ditch of ten, which is deep in proportion.

Upon the plot where the palace stood, but at thirty yards distance, is a broad circular

bank

bank ten yards diameter, which surrounds a hollow of not more than three, with an entrance on one side. This Rowland calls a Court of Justice, nor can I see any other use to which it could be appropriated. This being small, induces an idea, that disputes, and the violation of law, occurred so seldom, that a little court might suffice for a little business.

Here I found myself surrounded with water, which, trying to escape, I was again let in; thus I could better survey a ditch than jump over one.

I visited this place again September 1, 1800, when all the trenches were dry.

TAN BEN Y CEFN.

This lies upon a knob of earth about twenty yards above the fortification, which surrounds the Druid's palace, and is the ruins of a building, thirty yards long, and twenty broad, which Rowland and tradition call " The remainder of British houses;" it was divided into compartments. These ruins are the only stones upon the whole premises, and lie in confusion.

Having surveyed the Arch Druid's royal repository, I left the place, and rose the hill, giving back many a look at this venerable spot of antiquity, once, perhaps, the first in Great Britain, and arrived at the pleasant village of Bryn Siancyn, when my servant, whose ears were quicker than mine, remarked, " This is a methodist meeting, and " the minister is now preaching." It was Tuesday at noon. Ever at home, I stept in, and was surprized at seeing about two hundred devout attendants; a number, which I supposed the whole neighbourhood could not have produced. I heard a sermon, not one word of which I understood; saw some

some gestures in the preacher, which I could not approve, but could well allow, because I love freedom, and heard singing which delighted me.

LLANIDAN.

The worship ended, I asked several inhabitants " whether they understood English?" After many negatives, I was directed to the blacksmith, whom I knew had been my pious neighbour in the meeting, and seemed one of the most steady of the flock. I requested him to take me to that field in Llanidan, where the Romans landed, and murdered the Britons by thousands. He gave me the Welch name, now forgotten, which is, in English " The Field of Tears." Rowland calls it, " Meas Mawr Gad." " The " Great Armies Field." It lies three hundred yards from the Menai, and is about twenty acres.

acres. I knew they both meant the same. I found my pious blacksmith had left all his religion in the meeting-house against his return, for he treated me with plenty of good natured oaths.

I afterwards examined the other side of the Menai, and common sense informed me, the Romans entered the water about two hundred yards south of Llanfair-iscar church, the shore being here the flattest, the water the shallowest, and only three quarters of a mile wide; but at low *water*, and a neap tide, most of the bed is dry; so that the Romans would have only one or two small channels to swim over.

After the death of Nero, in the year 67, the natives having borne the Roman yoke six years, threw it off, the Druids returned, assumed their authority, property, and pride, which they held till the year 76, when Agricola crossed the Menai nearly a mile farther north,

north, landed at a field yet called Pont yr Scraphie (Bridge of Boats) where the same tragedy was acted, in that, and the two adjoining fields, Llania-lywyon, and Bryn Ladler, as was acted sixteen years before.

THE CARNEDD.

The tombs of the great have, in all ages, drawn the eye of the curious. Here he contemplates the rise and the zenith of glory, and here he contemplates the fall. That animated body of which the world stood in awe, and which held the keys of life and death, is now of no more consequence than the dirt, and the pebbles that cover it. When I held one of the principal bones of Humphry Duke of Glocester in my hand, I could not forbear reflecting what it *was* and what it *is*. Neither could I survey the tomb of Edward the First, without considering, it inclosed what once held the whole kingdom in vassalage, and was the terror of Wales and of Scotland.

I now travelled about three miles along the banks of the Menai, to Plas Newydd, anciently Llwyn Moel (the Wood on the Hill, or rather, the Church on the Hill) a seat of Lord Uxbridge, nor can I see any reason for abrogating the old name, which was more expressive than the new, for on this hill was one of the principal groves in the island sacred to Druidical worship.

The first object I approached was the Carnedd, or place of burial. It once covered a space of ground one hundred and forty-two yards in circumference, raised into a pyramid with common stones, evidently broken for the purpose, because they are rather sizable, at a medium, that of a large fist, thrown promiscuously together, and mixed with soil to favour

favour the growth of timber, a covering which added to the venerable aspect.

The Carnedds were of various sizes; this was very large, but to what height raised, is uncertain. It would well bear fifty feet. An aperture was left for admission. Time, and the rude fingers of man, are enemies to the productions of the ancients. One of the recent proprietors of these once sacred regions, not suspecting relics within, but taking this mouldering mound for a heap of rubbish, began to level it, but meeting with human bones, ordered the workmen to desist, which left the Carnedd in its present state—which is

A bank about two thirds of the above circumference, fourteen feet high, composed of stones covered with grass, and here and there a tree. The bank is also sloped down on the inside, in the form of a bowl or dish. At the bottom of this hollow lies a flat stone, six feet square,

square, which, supported, at one end, and two sides, by upright stones, leaves an opening at the other end that a man might creep into. At the far end is another stone, which lies in the same state, and was for the same use, but is only about four feet square. By the side of these, but at six yards distance, are the marks of another, now totally demolished.

A certain trait, by which we may judge of the manners of a departed people, is the monuments they have left us. By the Carnedd we see the Britons paid great attention to their dead.

In Llanfair church-yard, above-mentioned, the traveller may be treated with the sight of a modern Carnedd, now in use, the depository of the family of Wynn. A rude heap of stones of the size before described, has probably received the family for ages. It is five feet high, twelve wide, and eighteen long.

long. In the centre is the stump of a large old tree, worn out with age, and towards the south end a gigantic yew, which having watched over the dead a few centuries, is itself in a dying state. This proves the tumulus is of some antiquity. The entrance, according to the old Jewish fashion, as well as British, is guarded by a stone.

THE CROMLECH.

This altar of death was probably in use many ages prior to the christian æra, and many centuries prior to the extinction of Druidical worship. It excites a melancholy idea, when we consider the vast number of lives, both of the human and brute creation, which have been sacrificed upon this fatal stone! We should naturally ask, " Is that *religion* which delights in blood! Can that man be a proper *minister* of religion, whose

daily

daily practice is cutting throats! And can that people, who delight in the spectacle, be any other than savages?" It would still increase the sorrowful idea, if the cruel lesson, taught by *that* generation is, even in a small degree, applicable to this.

Two hundred yards north of the Carne*dd*, and the same distance from the Menai, stands the compleatest Cromlech in Anglesea, perhaps in Great Britain. The cap-stone of this ancient British monument is twelve feet long in the centre, and ten broad.

On one side it is twelve feet and a half long, and only eight on the other. A corner seems always to have been wanting.

The head or upper end of this stone, which lies flat, and points towards the east, is, in the thickest part, four feet and a half, and the other, or lower end, three and a half. This difference in the thickness causes a declension at one end *without*, but *within* the height is equal.

equal. Some of the upper part seems to have been split off, perhaps by the repeated heat of the fires, by the rains, and the thaws, for there appears one or two small steps.

This amazing weight *was* supported by seven upright stones, four feet high, or rather the irregular points of seven, now five, for two are down; one lies within the place, by way of seat, and the other rears sloping, near the foot. Three of these stones support the head, or broad end of the cap-stone; one is four feet and a half thick, one three and a half, and one two and a half. The centre stone of the three seems to have been split by time; and the severed part gives no assistance. The lower end has but two uprights to support it, the other two being down, which opens a wide entrance; one is three feet thick, and the other only two. One of these two seems to yield to the pressure.

It may give a clear idea of this Druidical construction, which has weathered out more than two thousand years, to suppose it the inside of a small room, four feet high, and six wide, supported as above, by five stones.

As the Cromlech stands on the declivity of an eminence, the cap-stone, on one side, is only two feet from the ground, that ground being also a little elevated, but on the other, and within, four feet, as already mentioned. The floor, which is soil, being a little hollowed with modern use, I suppose will admit a man of five feet to stand upright within.

Eleven inches from the lower end stands a much smaller Cromlech, and which once joined it, because a piece, of perhaps four hundred weight, seems to have been broken off, and caused a separation.

The whole height of this is five feet, once supported by five stones, now four, two feet high. The cap-stone is four feet and a half
by

by five and a half, and nearly three feet thick.

The wind, in a long course of ages, having deposited a small dust upon the upper surface of these awful relics, has encouraged the vegetable growth, and this growth made a lodgement for more, so that the tops are now nearly covered with soil, and that with flowers, fern, grass, briars, &c. which adds to the solemnity of the aspect.

A plot of ground, on the upper side, has been inclosed for the use of the Cromlechs, of which they form exactly one square, about eighteen feet. The building is wholly of a hard blue slate, a native of the country. The stones were used just as they were formed by nature, and surrounded, as all their sacred places were, with a thick grove of oaks, called Llwyn, hence the word Llan, Church.

Much conjecture has been spent upon these venerable pieces of antiquity. But I have no doubt of the greater Cromlech being appropriated

appropriated for the sacrifice; the lesser, for the use of the priest, while he attended it; the inclosure, to secure the victims till wanted; and its elevation, to facilitate their approach to the summit of the altar.

OWEN TUDOR.

To taste *only* of a favourite dish, excites, in a hungry man, a longing for more. Thus Pennant, in his Tour through Anglesea, *only* mentioning that Plas Penmynidd was the native place of Owen Tudor, excited a wish for a minute enquiry.

It may be thought singular for a man of seventy-seven, to spend two days, and walk thirty-three miles to examine the place, and make that enquiry.

The chief that is said of Owen, in history, is, " that he was accomplished, and a hand-
" some

"some Welch gentleman." And is this all the man merits who furnished England with a numerous race of kings! Shall he be consigned to oblivion whom history has not charged with error, but loaded with evils? Let him live then in my page, as he has not found another.

Penmynidd is situated in Anglesea, upon the great post road from London to Holyhead, six miles beyond Bangor Ferry. Whether he was Lord of the Manor, does not appear, but I am inclined to think he was, because he possessed the Manor House—Plas in Welch signifies Hall in English.

His private estate was not quite four hundred acres; worth, in the present day, seven and six-pence an acre, one hundred and fifty pounds per annum. As money, three hundred and seventy-eight years ago, was ten times the value it is now, his estate must then have been about fifteen pounds a year.

The

The two sums were equal in *real* though not in *nominal* value, and would equally constitute a gentleman. He occupied his own estate.

The land, at Plas Penmynidd, forms the side of a hill, and declines to the west. Some part, I am told, is worth a guinea an acre, and some half a crown.

The house is stone, unhewn, the walls of which are three feet thick, and stands in the grounds, about two hundred yards from the road, but fronting the north, and consists of only two stories, four rooms on a floor, all low, and little. Such a house, I believe, might be erected, in the present day, for three hundred pounds. Tradition says, " It " has been rebuilt since Owen's time." And Pennant says, " There is a gate-way and a chimney-piece yet standing." But tradition may mistake *repairing* for *building*; and Pennant's gate-way is certainly a common house-door,

door, without a porch, three feet wide, and forms a gothic arch. The thick wall being cyphered off, and fluted in the gothic stile, gives it a grander air. To this you rise by a semi-circular flight of four steps.

The chimney-piece is ample, of hewn stone, an elliptic arch, and in tolerable perfection. It is contracted within, perhaps owing to smoak, and the room, dignified by Pennant with " The Great Hall." It would better bear that of *the kitchen*, for I think it is not fifteen feet square, and unpaved.

A small modern addition, or two, seems to have been made to the back part of the house, facing the turnpike road. If the door and chimney-piece are allowed to be Owen's, we must allow the whole, except as above, for there is not the least appearance of *new* being joined to *old*. A roof cannot be expected to endure three hundred and fifty years; but when stone walls, three feet thick,

thick, are kept dry, and fresh pointed, as the frost destroys the mortar, who can say how long they will *not* last. The house, the steps, &c. I have no doubt, were erected by Owen, as soon as he could put his hand into the queen's pocket.

Over the house-door, is a device cut in stone, too much weather beaten to understand. Over the stable door, the family arms. In the wall of the brewhouse, are five stones, with inscriptions. On one, *Eslopus*—another, *ausdod* (the first letter wanting.) On a third, *Vivelu Vivas*. A fourth, consisting of eight or ten words, much hurt by time. The fifth, $\left.\begin{smallmatrix}B. & O.\\ E. & O.\end{smallmatrix}\right\}$ 1650. Perhaps the initials of two brothers who repaired the building. Upon a summer, within the brewhouse, fifteen feet long, is a line of words, in an ancient stile, the whole length of the beam, which I could not understand.

The estate is Lord Bulkeley's.

By

By what means Owen found his way to court, is uncertain, but at his first introduction, being silent, as unacquainted with the English tongue, he was called, "The dumb "Welchman." An indication of modesty, and a favourable trait in his character.

I shall state what traditions I could learn from elderly people, born upon the premises, and firmly believed by them, give my sentiments, and leave the reader to his.

While Owen, with others, was dancing with queen Catherine, his knee happened to touch her (tradition does not say he wore a knee-buckle, with a projecting tongue). He tied a ribbon about his knee, "Sir," says the Queen, "Why do you use that ribbon?" "Please your Grace, to prevent touching "you."—" But perhaps you may touch me "in another part."—Neither does tradition say, that her eyes spoke in plainer language than her tongue; language that could not be mistaken.

mistaken. Who can refuse to enter, when a beautiful sovereign opens the door!

The queen sent privately into Anglesea to enquire into particulars. Owen bribed the messengers, and apprized his mother of their errand.—" Arriving at Plas Penmynidd, they " found the mother dining on a dish of po- " tatoes upon her knee." To their interrogatories she replied " She fed upon *roast* and " *boiled* (potatoes cooked two ways) that she " would not take a hundred pounds for her " table (her knees) and that she kept six *male* " and six female servants, constantly under " arms for defence (goats with horns)."

When a man rises, like Owen, he stands as a butt for every one to shoot at. That the dance, the ribbon, the reply, and the bright intelligent eyes of the queen, may be true, there is little doubt. She must make the first advances. He durst not. But the roast, and boiled, the hundred pound table, the potatoes,

tatoes, and the goats, were probably sneers thrown at the man who had risen higher than themselves. And though I have no doubt of the old woman dining in the plain stile mentioned above, which was more consonant to the fashion of that day than this, yet it is certain that potatoes were then unknown in Anglesea.

Henry the Fifth died in 1422, leaving his son Henry the Sixth eight months old. Catherine married Owen in 1428, and by what we can gather from history, they lived agreeably with each other. She never acted upon the political stage, and he was kept totally behind the curtain, not having had conferred upon him even the honour of knighthood, till perhaps thirty years after, when dubbed by his son, the Earl of Pembroke. The king's uncle assumed the reigns of government, to whom this match was disagreeable.

P   The

The queen lived nine years after marriage, and died January 3, 1437, in Bermondsey. She was buried—but when Henry the Seventh, her grandson, built his chapel, she was taken up, and never interred after, but lay neglected in a shabby coffin, near her husband's monument, in Westminster Abbey.

During the next twenty-two years, Owen seems to have sunk in his stile of living, and in his resources, which perhaps were reduced to the issues of his estate. The queen seems to have been his protector, for upon her death, Humphry Duke of Gloucester, caused him to be apprehended, and committed to the tower, because, contrary to the statute made in the sixth of this king's reign (after the fault was committed) he had presumed to marry the queen without the king's consent.

He escaped out of this prison, but was again apprehended, and committed to Wallingford castle, under the Earl of Suffolk; out of which,

which, by the help of a priest, he made a second escape, but unfortunately was taken by Lord Beaumont, and a third time committed, and that to Newgate. Polychronicon says, " He was a squire of low birth, and as low degree." By this description, however, the reader will form a just idea of his mode of life. We all know, that Henry the Seventh, his grandson, could not rest till he had traced him up to the famous Cadwallader, and from him to the more famous Arthur, Prince of Wales.

By Catherine, Princess of France and Queen of England, Owen had three sons and one daughter. And though the court took no notice of the father, except to punish him, they did of the children; not from love, or interest, but because tinctured with royalty. Edmund was created Earl of Richmond, and married the heiress of the house of Beaufort, pretenders to the crown, after the reigning family.

family. He died in 1456, at about the early age of twenty-seven, leaving his son, afterwards, Henry the Seventh, fifteen weeks old. Jasper was Earl of Pembroke. Owen took a religious order, and the daughter died young.

In 1459, Henry the Sixth granted to Owen one hundred a year out of his manors of Falkston, Walton, and Bensted, in Kent; and the next year, some emoluments out of his Lordship of Denbigh, which is a proof of his poverty. But he enjoyed these only one year, for in 1461 he was taken prisoner by Edward the Fourth, at the battle of Mortimer's Cross, in fighting for the House of Lancaster as an officer under his son, the Earl of Pembroke, was carried to Hereford, suffered decapitation, without a trial, and lies buried in the Gray Friars Church.

Whether he was a gainer, or loser, by his elevation, the reader will determine. His

private

private fortune would supply every necessary of life, and something more—all beyond is pride.

Penmynedd, sterile in the growth of grass, has produced a plentiful growth of kings. Some of the princes of Europe originated here. From this solitary spot have arisen fourteen sovereigns, who swayed the British sceptre. From the old woman, who dined on potatoes upon the hundred pound table, is descended, in the thirteenth degree, George the Third, King of Great Britain.

Owen Tudor,
Edmund Tudor, Earl of Richmond,
Henry the Seventh,
Margaret, married to James IVth, King of Scotland,
James the Fifth, King of Scotland,
Mary, the unfortunate Queen of Scots,
James the First, King of Great Britain,
Elizabeth, married to Frederick Vth, Elector Palatine,
Sophia, Princess of Hanover,
George the First,
George the Second,
Frederick, Prince of Wales,
George the Third.

BEAUMARIS.

After paying my tribute to the unfortunate Owen Tudor, I arrived at Beaumaris, which I examined with attention and pleasure; it is a place of some magnitude, containing six or seven streets, and these populous. I was much delighted with the castle, but much more with Lord Bulkeley's premises, which join the town.—Pleased with my journey, I retreated over Bangor Ferry to Caernarvon.

By communicating with a people, an attachment commences, which *merit* increases; this will terminate in friendship; and when that occurs, we cannot separate without tender emotions. Something like this was felt during my stay at Caernarvon. Well treated by all, I was pleased *with* all. I have frequently

quently observed, that although I have only reposed one night at an inn, yet, from agreeable treatment and conversation, I found some regret the next day at parting. Though I saw the people but once, the mind revolted at the idea of seeing them no more. This was also the case at Bala. In one of my tours I stopped at the Three Golden Eagles (the arms of Wynn) where, by mistake, my saddle cloth was left. It was carefully preserved, though my return was not likely to happen.

In a subsequent tour, I received the cloth, but was sorry to find the unhappy landlord had been obliged to shut up. I then slept at the largest inn, I think the Lion, on the north side of the street, and the next morning experienced the painful feelings of a separation.

Without enquiring at Caernarvon what annual sums are appropriated for the repairs of a castle, past repairing? By what powers the place is governed? Or, by what interest a member finds a seat in Parliament? I must now quit the place, after some regret for every passing day.—The friendships contracted in two months will not be forgotten in two years.

I therefore leave this favourite place, and pass through Bangor. I must now cross the river Conway, about half a mile over. I was sorry that my poor horses must be flogged into a boat, for, to inflict punishment, without a fault, indicates brutality of mind. At a very small expence, the entrance might be made easy and expeditious, without the whip, or the hazard of a limb. This I pointed out to the boatmen, but might as well have addressed the boat. Old habits, though bad, are still favourite habits.

CHAP.

CHAP. XI.

St. Asaph — Denbigh — Ruthin — Mold — Offa's Dyke.

ST. ASAPH.

This is the sister city to Bangor, and, like that, consists of one short street, rises a hill, and has seventy-two houses. A man need not travel *over* the city to see it; he may do that while standing still. Nor can he say his eyes are offended with multitude, or his ears with sound.

Here, however, permit me to blazon the kindness of "Mine hostess, at the inn," who, because one half of my family were too much indisposed to eat, would not charge any thing for supper. This we would not allow, except she

she could prove that she had her house, furniture, food, fire, candles, and servants, for nothing.

As our road lay towards Chester, we debated whether we should veer to the left, and see that wonder-working water Holywell, famous for the rapidity of its stream, and the resort of folly, or to the right, and survey the more justly famed Vale of Clwyd, a spot of ground, or, meadow if you please, twenty-six miles long, and eight wide. We chose the last; and here a Welchman might have some reason to ask, " Is there a better in all " England?" The farms, I am told, let for three pounds per acre, and the produce is sixteen times more than supports the inhabitants. Though a valley, it is not wholly destitute of hills; St. Asaph, as above, stands upon one, Denbigh upon another, and Ruthin upon a third. Here too, the rich cloathing of mother earth covers the idleness of her sons. In other places, the peasant is too indolent to bring her into action, but here she acts from herself.

DENBIGH

Is populous, large, and pleasant, but upon too steep an ascent. The ruined castle is much more elevated. The prospect is delightful, overlooking this vast and charming meadow.

We descend the hill and enjoy a most beautiful ride to

RUTHIN,

A town of some consequence, upon the summit of a hill. On one whole side there is no approach, and it is accessible on the other by three streets, which, like the folds of a fan, terminate in one point, the market place. Here the eye is disgusted with the first object, a shattered, black, and disagreeable town hall,

hall, which stands in as bad a situation as art could fix it.

Close to the town are the ruins of a castle, now nearly level with the ground, but its foundations, and strength, are easily traced. This was erected by a branch of the ancient and powerful family of Grey, who acquired the lands by the sword, the strongest and basest title we know. It is now possessed by the family of Middleton of Chik. No title to an estate can be justified, except those of descent, gift, or contract. What should we think of the rectitude of a prince, who quarrels with a weaker state, and then gives his subjects leave to conquer, and inherit their property? Many of the best estates in Wales come under this description.

Travelling a mile from Ruthin, in our way to Mold, we rise Bwlch Pen Barras, being part of a vast chain of mountains which terminates the vale of Clwyd.

During

During our rise, we often turned to view the fine spot we were leaving. The day was clear, the sight magnificent.

Covering the mountain, we again beheld the ragged rocks of Wales.

MOLD

Is an agreeable and creditable place; has two spacious streets, which, with the inhabitants, are wholly in the English stile. Here both languages are spoken.

OFFA's DYKE.

Travelling one mile and a half on the Chester road, we come to this dyke, the ancient and famous boundary between Wales and England, extending from Basingwerk in Flintshire to Monmouth. The traveller would pass it unheeded, if not pointed out. All that remains is only a small hollow which runs along

along the cultivated fields, perhaps not eighteen inches deep in the centre, or more than twenty yards diameter.

When the Romans made their inroads into this island, about the commencement of the christian æra, many of the Britons were said to have retreated into Wales, at which time the rivers Dee, in the neighbourhood of Chester, and the Severn, divided the two countries. All to the east was England, and to the west Wales.

This division continued about six hundred years, when the ambitious and successful Offa, coveting the fertile lands of his neighbours, easily raised a quarrel, and an army, drove them westwards to the mountains, seized their property, formed this vast dyke, and ordained, that neither English nor Welchman should pass it.

Thus, he *divided*, instead of *uniting* man, promoted rancour instead of harmony, blood instead of peace. Modern cultivation is here hiding

hiding this monument of iniquity. Though curious to the eye of the antiquary, it fixes a badge of infamy on the man.——It must, however, be confessed, that Offa had the shadow of a reason for this depredation, for while his ambition prompted him to carry his arms against Alric, king of Kent, and Kenwulf, king of the West Saxons, to butcher the people, and subjugate the country, the princes of North and South Wales, uniting their power, in 776, made an attack upon his territories.——Thus innocent subjects fall a sacrifice to sovereign pride.

By this plunder Offa added to his dominions about one third of Wales, or, a piece of land about one hundred and thirty miles long, and of various diameters, for from Worcester to Presteign is about thirty-eight miles; from Bewdley to four miles beyond Bishop's Castle about forty; from Bridgnorth to four miles short of Welchpool thirty-two; and from Shrewsbury to Chirk twenty-four. Nearly half

half of Flintshire was afterwards re-annexed to Wales.

Having passed the dyke, I quitted, with regret, a people whose primitive manners were engaging, and whose country delighted me.

THE END.

INDEX.

	Page		Page
Aberistwith -	8	Cromlech - -	197
Adventures of a Shilling	10	Conway - -	58
——— with a Stranger	13	Canoffice - -	13
Astronomer's Stone	182	Castle, Caernarvon -	76
Asaph, St. - -	217	Coffin Joan Plantagenet's	114
Aber - - -	59	Capel Cerig - -	129
——— Church -	65	Conway, River -	58
Accidents - -	79	Cerig y Druidian -	55
Anglesea - -	177	Devil's Bridge -	5
Bishop's Castle -	2	Dinas Mouddy -	16
Barmouth - -	27	Dollgelly - -	27
Bwlch y Gwiddyl -	162	Dinas Dinlle - -	116
Bwlch yr Eistddfa -	164	Dol Badern Castle -	160
Bino, St. - -	119	Druidical Remains -	178
Bryn Gwyn - -	180	Denbigh - -	219
Bala - - -	37	De Broes - -	111
Bangor - -	65	Drws y Coed -	125
Bettus y Coed -	120	Dyke, Offa's -	2
Beddkelart - -	126	Eglwys Wrw -	33
Beaumaris - -	214	Ferries - -	177
Bridge, Devil's -	5	Fuel - -	85
Breos, William de	111	Festiniog - -	131
Caractacus - -	55	Goat, the - -	137
Cottage, the -	12, 22	Glyn Llgwy -	130
Cader Idris - -	26	Glendwr - -	48
Cross Hour -	132	Grey, Lord -	51
Caernarvon - -	72	Head of two Rivers	25
Old - - -	139	Joan Plantagenet -	113
Clynog - -	119	——— her Coffin -	114
Carnedd - -	193	Jumpers -	94

Q   Journey

INDEX.

	Page		Page
Journey to Caernarvon	103	Pont y Glin	38
Kerniogie	57	Passes, Five	73
Ludlow	2	Plantagenet, Joan, her coffin	114
Llanidloes	4	Plas Penmynidd	202
Llanvair	15	Rivers, Head of two	25
Llewellin	111	Roads	167
Llanberis	161	Rhiaidr Mowr	59
Llynieu Nanlle	125	Ruthen	219
Llanidan	191	Rhaiadr y Wenol	130
Land	136	Rug	53
—— Value	165	Sputty	4
Llanrwst	57	Sunday, to find	62
Llangollon	47	Snowdon	142
Llanlyfni	126	Tour from Birmingham to Caernarvon	103
Language, Welch	29	Tre'r Drwy Bach	183
Mold	221	Tre'r Dryw	187
Montgomery	3	Timber	86, 138
Malwyd	12	Tan Ben y Cefn	189
Market at Caernarvon	83	Tudor, Owen	202
New Town	3	Virtues of Plum Pudding	68
Nant Gwynan	173	Wrekin	39
Nant Frankon	174	Winifrid, St.	124
Offa's Dyke	2	Welch Wedding	87
Oswestry	41	Water	137
Oswald	41	Welch Language	29
Old Oswestry	43	Welch Pool	15
Owen Glendwr	48	Woman, Old, and Satan	7
Owen Tudor	202	Well, St. Beuno's	119
Old Caernarvon	139	Yew, the	21
Ogwen Pool	173		
Pudding, Plum	68		

SKETCHES

Of some of the mountainous Views in North Wales.

PLATE I.

Contains a view taken from near the summit of MOEL HEBOG, a mountain opposite to Beddkelart, from whence Snowdon and other hills from N. N. E. to E. S. E. are seen to great advantage. From this exalted situation the mountains do not assume that grand height as when they are seen from a less elevated station; but the view has abundant matter of compensation, by the extent and grandeur of the appearance below. The River Glaslyn is discovered winding through and watering the fertile small Vale of Nant Gwynan, and the Lakes Llyn-y-Dinas, and Llyn Gwynan, diversify and harmonize the scene, and the whole view terminates in a beautiful and immense picture.

PLATE II.

Represents Llewydd, Snowdon, and Crib Coch, as seen from Llyn Taurn, at the foot of Snowdon. It is impossible, by any description, to give even a faint idea of this magnificent view, which combines all that is grand, awful, and majestic. The king of mountains appears here, in all the terrific, superb, and lofty grandeur of Majesty, and is well supported by his gigantic attendants. In contemplating this vast and awful sight, the human mind feels the insignificance of man, with reverence looks through nature up to nature's God! and exclaims, " These are thy glorious Works, Parent of Good! Almighty!"

PLATE III.

PLATE III.

Exhibits a view taken from Festiniog Church-yard, and discloses a chain of mountains from N. W. by W. to E. by E. This grand prospect is not to be surpassed in natural beauty, and boldness of scenery; the rocky projections, deep glens, dreadful precipices, and wonderful cataracts, are truly characteristic of this wild and tremendous country, and the traveller feels a laudable propensity to examine these mighty regions, the sight of which fills his mind with amazement, and rivets the fancy to the delight of exploring the beauties of nature in its rudest and most fantastic form.

BOOKS by the same Author.

1. The HISTORY of BIRMINGHAM, 8vo. 7s. 6d.
2. The JOURNEY to LONDON, 12mo. 2s. 6d.
3. The COURT of REQUESTS, 8vo. 6s.
4. HISTORY of the HUNDRED COURT, being a Supplement to the Court of Requests, 8vo. 1s.
5. The HISTORY of BLACK POOL, frequented for Sea Bathing, 1s.
6. The BATTLE of BOSWORTH FIELD, 8vo. 5s.
7. The HISTORY of DERBY, 8vo. 7s.
8. The BARBERS, a Poem, 1s.
9. EDGAR and ELFLEDA, 8vo. 1s.
10. The HISTORY of the ROMAN WALL, 8vo. 7s.

NOV 3 0 1937

Check Out More Titles From HardPress Classics Series In this collection we are offering thousands of classic and hard to find books. This series spans a vast array of subjects – so you are bound to find something of interest to enjoy reading and learning about.

Subjects:
Architecture
Art
Biography & Autobiography
Body, Mind &Spirit
Children & Young Adult
Dramas
Education
Fiction
History
Language Arts & Disciplines
Law
Literary Collections
Music
Poetry
Psychology
Science
…and many more.

Visit us at www.hardpress.net

Im The Story
personalised classic books

"Beautiful gift.. lovely finish.
My Niece loves it, so precious!"

Helen R Brumfieldon
★★★★★

UNIQUE GIFT
FOR KIDS, PARTNERS AND FRIENDS

Timeless books such as:

Kids

Alice in Wonderland · The Jungle Book · The Wonderful Wizard of Oz
Peter and Wendy · Robin Hood · The Prince and The Pauper
The Railway Children · Treasure Island · A Christmas Carol

Adults

Romeo and Juliet · Dracula

- **Highly** Customizable
- **Change** Books Title
- **Replace** Characters Names with yours
- **Upload** Photo (for inside page)
- **Add** Inscriptions

Visit
ImTheStory.com
and order yours today!